VEGETABLES

VEGETABLES

*The Art of Growing, Cooking, and Keeping
the New American Harvest*

Colette Rossant
and
Marianne Melendez

PHOTOGRAPHS BY GREG SCLIGHT

Book Design by Ozubko Design

VIKING STUDIO BOOKS

VIKING STUDIO BOOKS

Published by the Penguin Group
Viking Penguin, a division of Penguin Books USA Inc.,
375 Hudson Street, New York, New York 10014, U.S.A.

Penguin Books Ltd, 27 Wrights Lane,
London W8 5TZ, England

Penguin Books Australia Ltd, Ringwood,
Victoria, Australia

Penguin Books Canada Ltd, 2801 John Street
Markham, Ontario, Canada L3R 1B4

Penguin Books (N.Z.) Ltd, 182–190 Wairau Road,
Auckland 10, New Zealand

Penguin Books Ltd, Registered Offices:
Harmondsworth, Middlesex, England

First published in 1991 by Viking Penguin,
a division of Penguin Books USA Inc.

10 9 8 7 6 5 4 3 2 1

LIBRARY OF CONGRESS CATALOGING IN PUBLICATION DATA

Rossant, Colette.

Vegetables : a growing wave/Colette Rossant and Marianne Melendez;
photographs by Greg Sclight.
p.   cm.
Includes index.
ISBN 0-670-82710-X
1. Cookery (Vegetables)
TX801.R794   1991   90–22428
641.6′5—dc20

Printed in Singapore

·

For Matthew James

·

CONTENTS

CONTENTS

ACKNOWLEDGMENTS

•

We thank Karen Kaplan of Frieda's, Inc., of California for sending us exquisite specimens of many vegetables and for her willingness to impart valuable information about unusual varieties.

Thanks, too, to Dean & DeLuca of New York for their loan of sundry dishes and glasses . . . and for their good taste.

Much gratitude to Contemporary Porcelain of New York for its loan of exquisite and completely original platters, bowls, and plates and for Lennie's generosity.

To the American potter Richard Millgrin, who resides in Kyoto, we owe much thanks for this loan of hand-crafted platters and bowls.

We are indebted as well to Malcolm Clark of California's Sonoma Valley for sending us his unique and perfect mushrooms.

Thanks to Jaimie Douglas of the Sonoma County Convention and Visitor's Bureau for being such a pleasant and informative liaison between us and the county's growers.

And, finally, our gratitude to our husbands, James and Jacques, for being on call with grace and good humor.

•

I was not born, as my mother was, holding a silver fork in one hand and a Sabatier knife in the other. And although my childhood weekend breakfasts included fried eggs, grits, and slab bacon (my father grew up in the South), and though my lunchbox was packed with pâté, my favorite food in fifth grade was the ubiquitous Yodel, which I carefully unrolled while watching "Dark Shadows" on television and ate tiny bite by tiny bite at Mary Bailey's house. Whenever she came to my house, our after-school snack consisted of English muffins spread thinly (my father was also a child of the Depression) with sour orange marmalade. I always went to Mary Bailey's house.

Vegetables were handled well, I even admitted it then, by my mother. Served in pristine solitude—my siblings and I would balk if peas were mixed with carrots—the broccoli or green beans or Brussels sprouts were fresh and never overcooked. I ate them first, as most children do, saving the best, a sizzling lamb chop or chicken leg, for last.

That is, until I met Melon. I mean Alan. I just called him Melon. He shared my birthday and listened to my problems and never let on that he was twenty years older than I. One summer, when I was twelve, Alan spent a long weekend with the family on Long Island. He was a budding gourmet cook when there weren't many around and decided that he would make Saturday night's dinner. Well, his girlfriend went into a huff, since this meant precious time away from romance on the beach, and my mother rolled her eyes, knowing that there was precious little in the fridge. I, on the other hand, eagerly volunteered to be his helper. It was five o'clock: Alan and I marched into the primitive kitchen and closed the door behind us. I opened the refrigerator door and whined, "There's nothing to eat!"

It wasn't true, but for a twelve-year-old, "food" means something other than fresh vegetables with the earth still on them. Alan, however, was gleeful. He took the entire crisper out of the fridge and ordered me to peel everything in it while he *stepped out into the neighboring potato field to dig up a few baby tubers. The crisper contained a couple of limp carrots, a head of lettuce, a few ripe tomatoes, cooked green beans left over from the night before, and a mesh bag of shallots. Alan returned, sautéed lots of chopped shallots in butter, added the cut-up vegetables, some canned broth, and some fresh herbs, all the while singing Bette Midler's "You've Got to Have Friends" with his slightly off-key but pleasant tenor. After about twenty minutes or so of simmering, the whole mess was tossed into a Cuisinart and whirred into a smooth puree. Alan then stuck the soup back into the fridge, chopped the heart of the lettuce very fine, and mixed everyone some gin and tonics (even me!). At seven, he said, "À table," and we sat down (I was rather smashed) to bowls of chilled garden soup sprinkled with chopped lettuce and hot croutons. We toasted Alan, Alan toasted me, and I brought out my rhubarb pie, made that morning, happier than a lark.*

Melon was riding the cusp of a new wave that my mother and I jumped on immediately. And from that moment on we have never stopped exploring the world of vegetables.

It was like a fever, once we realized that we were in unexplored territory. I suppose that New York City's Chinatown was the first stop on our quest. From its crowded maze came a grand array of produce—fuzzy melon, wood ear mushrooms, taro root—challenging us to create meals of colorful complexity. I clamored for my mother's Chinese flowering cabbage, bathed in a lemony sauce and topped with black and white sesame seeds. I tried my hand with long beans, braising them with pork chops and unpeeled garlic cloves. From Chinatown, Colette and I went our separate ways, as mothers and daughters are wont to do. She wandered off to California, following a trail of miniature squash and baby corn, edible flowers, haricots verts and pom pom blanc mushrooms. She traveled to South America, where mild chayote inspired her to invent piquant vegetable sauces. She visited farmers in Florida, upstate New York, and Pennsylvania, sniffing out the experiments, the risks, the gems that grew from carefully tilled and treated soil.

I followed my roots (animal—human, that is—as well as vegetable) to France, the ultimate culinary classroom. I stayed there for four years, long enough to toss pousse pied (salicornia) about my kitchen counter as if it were as mundane as garlic. I learned how to peel a truffle, blanch asparagus, stew cardoons, and wash leeks. When I returned to the

States (with a French husband to keep me on my cooking toes), my mother and I found that we had arrived at the same conclusion: expanding, enriching, and developing American cuisine depended on vegetables. But how?

By allowing vegetables to set the entire tone of a meal. How much more varied, colorful, textured, and adaptable vegetables are than meat, fish, or fowl. We would set them up first, switching roles so that the spinach would be adorned with lamb, the Romanesco cauliflower complemented by fried smelts. Or we would simply let the vegetables reign alone, making each dish unique, so that the usual main course would never be missed. Of course, we had our individual approaches to this challenge. I tend to be the traditionalist, bringing back long-forgotten gratins and hearty soups, simple purees and main-course salads. My mother is like a mad scientist with artistic inclinations: she combines taro with Stilton, cardoons with clementines, leeks with seaweed. Need I go on?

The second part of our mission consisted of "discovering" unusual vegetables and finding ways to incorporate them into our cuisine. We stuffed elephant garlic with pesto cream cheese and made a salad of cactus leaves, all the while urging avant-garde and new-age growers to continue their experiments and widen their distribution.

Finally, we were ready to give birth to this book. The recipes came naturally enough; in the kitchen, my mother and I work with a smoothness and cooperation that are missing even in some of the greatest restaurant kitchens of the world. But when it came to revealing our thoughts on each vegetable, our relationship took the upper hand. After all, we are mother and daughter and don't see eye to eye on most things. So each chose to write about the vegetables that she felt most strongly about. Sometimes, we were moved to respond to one another, but mostly we found ourselves loyal to particular vegetables. In order for the reader to recognize our musings as mine or my mother's, a different typeface is used for each.

Vegetables are a growing wave in America. From the sandy loam of Dade County, Florida, to the rich, black earth of California's Sonoma Valley, farmers are producing wondrous strains of vegetables. Collette and I—always hungry, always dreaming—have gathered up these strains and run with them.

MUSHROOMS

Marianne complains that I put mushrooms into everything. She thinks that I became obsessed with mushrooms after I came back from Japan. She is wrong. I never used to like mushrooms until I met Malcolm Clark, the mushroom man, who taught me how exquisite wild mushrooms could be. Only later did I go to Japan to taste matzutake mushrooms—smoky, woodsy, worth their weight in gold. I must point out, however, that Malcolm Clark is the one who introduced them to America.

Malcolm is the sort of man that might be considered an adventurer, or a swaggerer, or a pioneer—a man who plunges into any activity without fear and with a certain passion. He has held many fascinating jobs and has accomplished many intriguing feats. Nowadays, Malcolm Clark grows mushrooms. Of course, his mushrooms are not ordinary mushrooms. They have names like shiitake, pom pom blanc, hen-of-the-woods, trompette de la mort, pleurotte, and cinnamon cap. And they are artfully packed into blue boxes and decorated with a star made of fresh laurel leaves. How did an Englishman named Malcolm Clark, a former zoologist, marine biologist, and osteologist, end up cultivating mushrooms in California's Sonoma Valley?

I met Malcolm on a hot summer's day when his walnut trees were laden with fresh, ripe nuts. He is a tall, handsome man in his late thirties with the aura of an overgrown teddy bear and a formidable strength. His English accent seems out of place in such a purely American setting. I sat in his office in a corner of a large hangar, where several people were carefully packing large shiitake mushrooms, six to a box. Malcolm told me of his first job overseas as a game reserve worker. Later, he was off to Portugal, where, for ten months, he worked as a diver off the coast. He traveled in his free time—to Spain,

Chanterelle

Nameko

Portobello

Hen-of-the-woods

Pom pom blanc

Pleurotte

Porcino

Shiitake

Morel

◄ Fragrant, high-quality shiitake grow directly on the walls of a shed at a gourmet mushroom farm owned and run by one of Sonoma Valley's most innovative growers, Malcolm Clark. Pickers must use a ladder to reach the highest mushrooms, six to eight feet in the air.

Malcolm Clark, right, with chef Mark Malicki in Truffles, a restaurant in Sonoma Valley's major town of Sebastopol. Here, American regional cuisine shows off the valley's superb mushrooms.

Morocco, Tangiers, Marrakesh. He then was asked to spend the following two years in Caracas, Venezuela, working as a zoologist for the National Geographic Society. When he arrived in Caracas, he discovered that the expedition had been called off. He emigrated to Canada, and eventually became Director of Biological Research at Science Kit, a large American biological supply company. His newfound success and an avid interest in judo took Malcolm to Japan, where his life took an unexpected—and uncanny—turn toward the indomitable mushroom.

Malcolm tasted mushrooms that he had never known existed: the smoky matzutake mushroom, the tiny, spicy nameko, the saucer-shaped shiitake. With his scientific background, Malcolm realized that some of these mushrooms could be grown in a controlled environment. Intrigued by the commercial possibilities he saw in mushroom cultivation, he began to entertain thoughts of becoming a new-age farmer.

Back in Canada, Malcolm joined a group of Japanese-Canadians who had decided to grow shiitake mushrooms commercially. Malcolm experimented with new mushroom spores and, in no time, was made vice president of their fledgling company. Then he met Dr. Tsumeto Yoshi, a leading Japanese mushroom scientist who was developing a process to grow matzutake mushrooms commercially. Dr. Yoshi turned out to be Malcolm's mentor, a twist of fate since Dr. Yoshi was once a student of a disciple of Malcolm's great-great-grandfather, who had taught agriculture in Hokkaido and had been famous for imparting a sense of ambition to his pupils.

By now, mushroom fever was boiling in Malcolm's veins. In Science Kit's labs, Malcolm developed a process by which he grew Chinese coral mushrooms from golf-ball size to tennis-ball size. Every night, he could be found in his kitchen trying different ways of preparing these mushrooms. He began to be obsessed by mushrooms—he even admits that "I'm married to my occupation and my mushrooms won't let me go!"—and he dreamed of growing morels and trompettes de la mort in a controlled laboratory environment. He read books about mushrooms, talked mushrooms, ate mushrooms. At this point, his employers gave him an ultimatum: was he going to do research for the company or for mushrooms? Malcolm didn't hesitate long. The idea that science and nature could interact on an essential and daily basis to produce an edible, beautiful, and, above all, new creation captured Malcolm's imagination.

Malcolm's mushroom lab looks as if it were operating in the year 2002. The mushrooms are grown in cubes made of cellulose material and peat moss, out of which the mushroom nodules emerge, looking like small science fiction monsters with feelers. Although people thought at first that Malcolm was trying to poison them, the shiitake caught on. It has become the chic spore, an alternative to the white, and quite tasteless, button mushrooms so common in America. From fresh chanterelles to the newly developed Clam Shell mushroom—Malcolm's trademark for honshimeiji mushrooms—Malcolm produces magnificent specimens. Several secret specimens, still nameless, perfume the stark laboratory hangars. "One day I will cover America with mushrooms!" Malcolm claims emphatically. And I'm sure he will.

There are many varieties of wild mushrooms that hug the ground near oak and pine trees in forests throughout much of the United States, where they are gathered by farmers and mushroom devotees. They stalk open fields, cemeteries, decaying logs, and moss clumps as well. Many of these wild mushrooms are also cultivated in controlled environments, where they flourish atop synthetic materials in perfectly suited atmospheres. The most readily found in produce markets are cèpes (also called boletes and porcini), portobello mushrooms, morels, chanterelles, pleurottes (also called oyster mushrooms), shiitake mushrooms, trompettes de la mort, and hen-of-the-woods mushrooms.

Whenever either of us mentions white mushrooms in a recipe, we are talking about cultivated white mushrooms. These are available year round in supermarkets and gourmet produce stores. There are two types of cultivated mushrooms: one is pure white and smooth, the other is either off-white or light tan, with a more pronounced flavor. It is always better to buy loose mushrooms, which you can choose one by one, rather than those packed en masse in a plastic box. Choose firm, round mushrooms whose caps hug the stem and are devoid of black spots, which indicate age. Cultivated mushrooms lack aroma, yet, when cooked whole or sliced, they add a distinctive flavor to meat, fish, or poultry. They can be eaten raw, stewed, sautéed, baked, broiled, or stuffed.

Both wild and cultivated mushrooms should be refrigerated and eaten as soon as possible. They should not be peeled or washed extensively. They should be either wiped clean with a cloth or quickly rinsed under cold running water, then drained. The stems of most mushrooms, wild and cultivated, can be eaten, except for shiitake and nameko. Mushroom stems are excellent for making soups, consommés, or sauces.

Most mushrooms are also available dried or canned. Canned cultivated mushrooms have very little taste compared to preserved wild mushrooms in glass jars. Canned mushrooms should be drained, then added to a dish just before the end of cooking. The best preserved mushrooms in a jar are cèpes, porcini (these are also available frozen), and chanterelles.

Dried mushrooms, whether shiitake mushrooms, porcini, chanterelles, or morels, should be soaked in lukewarm water for at least an hour before using. Drain and pat dry with paper towels. The water in which mushrooms have soaked can be used as a base for soups or for basting a roast. First strain the mushroom water through a very fine mesh strainer. Once soaked, dried mushrooms can be used the same way as fresh ones.

Most recipes for wild mushrooms are interchangeable and can also be made with cultivated white mushrooms.

Ready for nationwide shipment, round, snowy white pom poms blancs, black-and-white hen-of-the-woods, and fragile pleurottes create a unique vegetable collage.

GOLD OR WHITE CHANTERELLE, OR HORN OF PLENTY

The trumpet-shaped caps of these mushrooms range in color from white to salmon to muddy brown to almost black. The chanterelle's cap measures from one to three inches in diameter, and has a fragrant and sometimes fruity taste. Small chanterelles are called girolles. Both come to the United States from France and Italy as well as from America's Pacific Northwest, where they are gathered in the wild. Recently, they have been cultivated in controlled environments in the United States. Chanterelles should be eaten as soon as possible after purchase. They should not be washed or sliced. If they are sandy, rinse them briefly under cool running water and pat dry with paper towels. They are best sautéed in butter with fresh herbs.

AVAILABILITY:
August to November; sometimes in winter in specialty stores.

SHOPPING GUIDE:
Select firm and fresh-looking chanterelles. Avoid those that seem damp or spotted.

STORAGE:
Will keep for 1 to 2 days, in a sealed plastic bag, in the refrigerator.

Fricassee of Chanterelles

◆ ◆ ◆

3 tablespoons butter

2 pounds white or gold chanterelles

Salt and pepper

8 colossal California black olives, pitted

1 ounce pickled red ginger*

2 ounces arugula, washed and drained

*Available in most Chinese or Japanese grocery stores.

In a large skillet, melt the butter. Add the chanterelles and sauté for several minutes over medium heat. Sprinkle with salt and pepper. Remove from the heat. ❖ Stuff the olives with the pickled ginger. ❖ Divide the mushrooms among 4 individual serving plates. Garnish with several stuffed olives and arugula and serve. ❖ Yield: 4 servings

The woodsy aroma of these gently sautéed chanterelles is enhanced by the fresh taste of uncooked arugula. Red pickled ginger adds piquancy and color. ▶

NAMEKO, OR CINNAMON CAP

I first saw nameko mushrooms in a Japanese open market, their small, brown caps displayed on red and gold oak leaves. When I picked one of the slightly slimy mushrooms to taste, the farmer behind the stand gestured wildly that I should refrain from putting it to my mouth. I complied, mystified. That evening, I described what had happened to a Japanese friend and she explained that the nameko are poisonous when eaten raw. She relieved my disappointment by offering me a silken consommé prepared with nameko, altogether delicious compensation.

Nameko, which grow exclusively in Japan and in Malcolm Clark's hothouse, are clusters of brown caps atop long, white inedible stems. Each cap is only about a quarter of an inch in diameter. They are best eaten as soon after purchase as possible. Nameko mushrooms are also available canned in Japanese grocery stores. When using canned namekos, rinse them under cold water to remove the broth that they are packed in. Use them in soups or sauté with fresh herbs.

AVAILABILITY:
October to February.

SHOPPING GUIDE:
Select shiny, fresh-looking caps. Avoid those with shriveled stems.

STORAGE:
Will keep for 2 to 3 days, loosely wrapped in plastic, in the refrigerator.

These mushrooms will be shipped still growing on their man-made cubes of cellulose.

Malcolm Clark will not reveal the nature of his growing material, but we know now that it produces wondrous results, as shown in these pom poms blancs and cinnamon caps.

To create a springtime feeling on a plate, we alternate delicate sunflower sprouts with tiny nameko mushrooms, forming a circle around a mound of clam seviche flavored with fresh coriander.

Nameko Mushrooms with Clams

• • •

In New York City's Chinatown, where we often shop, most fishmongers sell fresh tiny clams. Marinated for 24 hours in lime juice, these clams are superb when served with sautéed mushrooms. In this recipe, we use nameko mushrooms because their small caps resemble the clams themselves. Of course, any wild mushrooms can be used.

1 pound tiny clams, shucked, or

2 4-ounce jars clams in juice, drained

Juice of 2 limes

Freshly ground pepper

1 tablespoon chopped fresh coriander

1/2 pound fresh, or 2 4-ounce cans, nameko mushrooms

2 tablespoons olive oil

Salt

1/2 tablespoon chopped fresh chervil

1/2 cup (1 ounce) sunflower sprouts*

*Available in health-food stores.

Place the clams in a bowl and pour the lime juice over them. Add pepper to taste. Add the coriander, toss, and refrigerate for a minimum of 2 hours. ❖ *Separate the nameko caps from the central stem. In a skillet, heat the oil. Add the mushrooms and sauté over medium heat for several minutes. Remove from the heat, season with salt and pepper, and add the chervil. Stir gently.* ❖ *Divide the clams among 4 individual serving plates. Scatter the nameko over the clams or arrange as in photo. Garnish with the sprouts, and serve.*
❖ Yield: 4 servings

PORTOBELLO

The portobello is an enormous flying-saucer-shaped mushroom. Its dark brown cap is smooth and thick and tops a long, tough stem. Its aroma is woodsy and pungent. And I thank Lee Grimsbo for introducing it to me and to New York.

Lee Grimsbo is a tall man in his early thirties who hails from Minnesota. His father was a horticulturist well known in his field; from an early age, Lee took an interest in plant life and unusual produce. Although he intended to pursue a career in the arts, his passion for vegetables led him in a different direction. He began to help farmers in many parts of the country to grow and distribute native American vegetables that had become extinct. He also introduced New Yorkers to "new" vegetables from abroad. Today, Lee Grimsbo runs Manhattan Fruitiers, a concern that sells special gift baskets filled with unusual varieties of fruit and vegetables.

One day Lee, knowing how much I love wild mushrooms, showed me portobello mushrooms he had just received from Italy. For a moment, I wasn't sure they were real. But when he prepared them that night for my husband and me, I was happy they *were* real. He brushed them with olive oil and broiled them. Their taste and texture are reminiscent of a tender, broiled filet mignon. We made a mushroom consommé with the stems—dark, flavorful, delicious!

You can find imported portobellos in some gourmet produce shops; they are also grown in parts of Pennsylvania. These are not as large as the Italian ones but are just as thick and pungent. Mushrooms should always be eaten as soon after buying them as possible. Allow one per person.

◄ Imported from Italy, portobello mushrooms are so meaty and rich that they can be enjoyed broiled with just a brushing of olive oil. A cross cut into each mushroom cap allows the oil to penetrate the pungent flesh.

AVAILABILITY:
December to March.

SHOPPING GUIDE:
Select mushrooms with firm and smooth caps. Avoid those that are wrinkled, bruised, or broken.

STORAGE:
Will keep for 2 days, loosely wrapped in plastic, in the refrigerator.

Broiled Portobello Mushrooms with Garlic Bread

◆ ◆ ◆

4 portobello mushrooms

¼ cup extra-virgin olive oil

Salt and pepper

½ pound white mushrooms

8 tablespoons (1 stick) butter

3 shallots, peeled and chopped

1 cup dry white wine

½ cup chicken stock

1 tablespoon dried tarragon

¼ cup heavy cream (optional)

1 loaf garlic bread
(see recipe, page 18)

4 sprigs fresh coriander

Cut the stem off each portobello and set aside. Wipe caps with damp paper towel. With the point of a knife, cut a double cross—like a number sign—on the caps. Brush with olive oil, sprinkle with salt and pepper, and set aside. ❖ *Cut the stems off the white mushrooms and coarsely chop stems and caps. Trim the stems of the portobellos and coarsely chop. In a large skillet, melt the butter. Add the shallots and sauté until transparent; add the white mushrooms and the chopped portobello stems. Cook for 2 minutes, stirring constantly, then add the wine, stock, tarragon, cream (if desired), and salt and pepper to taste. Cook over low heat until reduced by half, 3 to 4 minutes. Set aside.* ❖ *Broil the portobello caps, top side up, for 5 minutes.* ❖ *Place 1 cap on each of 4 plates, spread with some sauce, and garnish with a thick slice of garlic bread and a sprig of coriander.* ❖ *Yield: 4 servings*

Broiled Portobello Mushrooms with Avocado-Tomatillo Sauce

. . .

This dish derives much of its flavor from Chinese chives – long, flat, dark green leaves about ¼ inch wide. They are sometimes called garlic chives. Their flavor is more intense than that of regular chives. Used sparingly, they add zest to many vegetables.

4 portobello mushrooms

3 tablespoons soy sauce

2 tablespoons melted butter

2 tablespoons extra-virgin olive oil

Salt and pepper

4 ounces Chinese or garlic chives

1 cup avocado-tomatillo sauce
(see recipe, page 268)

1 loaf garlic bread (see recipe ▶)

Trim the stems of the portobellos and wash under cold running water. Pat dry with paper towel before storing in a sealed plastic bag. Store or freeze for later use (they impart a rich flavor to a stew or chicken stock). Brush the tops of the mushrooms with the soy sauce and set aside. ❖ *Mix together the butter and oil. Season with salt and pepper to taste and set aside. Steam the chives for 2 minutes and cool to room temperature.* ❖ *Line a broiler with foil and place the mushroom caps on the foil, top side up. Brush with the butter-oil mixture and broil for 4 minutes, basting often.* ❖ *Arrange a bed of Chinese chives on each of 4 individual serving plates. Place a mushroom on top and a slice of garlic bread to the side. Serve with the avocado-tomatillo sauce.* ❖ *Yield: 4 servings*

....

Garlic Bread

. . .

This is *not* your ordinary garlic bread—the one made from a split Italian loaf slathered with butter and minced garlic, then broiled. This quick bread has garlic baked inside, along with lots of fresh herbs and olive oil, so it's light, fragrant, and unusual. Eat it with bean soups, grilled fish, or with a spoonful of sun-dried tomato spread.

10 cloves garlic, peeled

½ cup extra-virgin olive oil

¼ cup vegetable oil

1 teaspoon salt

2 eggs

1¼ cups flour

1½ teaspoons baking powder

½ cup milk

3 tablespoons minced herbs (basil, parsley, chervil, or a combination)

Preheat oven to 350 degrees.
❖ *In a food processor, puree the garlic, ¼ cup olive oil, the vegetable oil, and the salt. Add the eggs and process until smooth.* ❖ *Sift together the flour and baking powder. Add the flour mixture by spoonfuls to the garlic and oil, alternately with the milk, while the machine is running. Transfer to a greased loaf pan.* ❖ *Process minced herbs and remaining ¼ cup olive oil until well blended.* ❖ *Pour the herb-oil mixture on top of the batter in two vertical lines. With the blade of a dinner knife, cut through the batter using a swirling movement so that the herbed oil marbles the batter. Bake for 1 hour, or until light and golden. Cool to room temperature before slicing.* ❖ *Yield: 6 servings*

....

Cooked tomatillos and avocado combine to create a buttery sauce to complement the rich taste of a grilled portobello mushroom set on a bed of Chinese chives. Garlic bread baked with fresh herbs rounds out the meal. ▶

HEN-OF-THE-WOODS

A smoky gray, black, and white mushroom that grows at the base of trees or stumps, hen-of-the-woods can be found growing in forests after heavy rainfall in the fall. When found in the woods, the mushroom is light brown with a touch of white on its edges. It's about three to five inches in diameter. In Malcolm Clark's hothouse, it looks more like the brain of a scientist. It is excellent sautéed in butter, in casseroles, or baked with fresh herbs.

AVAILABILITY:
Hothouse hen-of-the-woods mushrooms are available all year round.

SHOPPING GUIDE:
Select firm and fresh-looking mushrooms.

STORAGE:
Will keep for 3 to 4 days, loosely wrapped in plastic, in the refrigerator.

Pom poms blancs, hen-of-the-woods, and cinnamon cap mushrooms form a symphony of textures.

Sautéed Hen-of-the-Woods

• • •

This dish is elegant and should be served for lunch or brunch along with a good red Burgundy and hot French rolls.

4 whole hen-of-the-woods mushrooms

4 tablespoons butter

Salt and pepper

2 cloves garlic, peeled and minced

1 lemon, sliced

3 sprigs fresh mint

A wok is the perfect utensil for preparing tender hen-of-the-woods, since these unusual mushrooms benefit from brief cooking over high heat.

Trim the mushrooms and cut into bite-size pieces. In a skillet, melt the butter, add the mushrooms, and sauté for 5 minutes. Add salt and pepper to taste, garlic, and a few drops of lemon juice. Cook for another few minutes. ❖ *Transfer to a serving platter, garnish with lemon slices and mint leaves, and serve.* ❖ Yield: 4 servings

POM POM BLANC

Malcolm Clark discovered this immense puffball in a field and decided to reproduce it in his hothouse. After several tries, he succeeded in cultivating this lovely, white, feathery mushroom. He chose its name because it reminded him of the white paper pom poms that little girls used to make in his native England. His pom pom blanc is a round, soft, pure-white mushroom with a feathery exterior. The caps can reach nearly twelve inches in diameter, but are usually five to eight inches. This mushroom tastes excellent baked with melted butter and can also be stuffed or simply steamed.

AVAILABILITY:
All year round, peak season late summer and fall.

SHOPPING GUIDE:
Hothouse pom poms blancs are sold in clear plastic containers. Select firm but light-for-their-size, pure-white mushrooms. Avoid those with yellow or brown stains.

STORAGE:
Will keep for 4 to 5 days in its unopened container in the refrigerator.

The pom pom blanc should be cooked whole to preserve its unique shape and texture.

Baked Pom Poms Blancs

❖ ❖ ❖

Malcolm Clark believes that the best way to cook these delicate mushrooms is to bake them in a hot oven with melted butter so as not to spoil their texture. We tried several different recipes and found Malcolm's to be the best.

8 pom poms blancs

4 tablespoons melted butter

Salt and freshly ground pepper

1/2 cup (1/2 ounce) garden cress
or radish sprouts

Preheat the oven to 450 degrees.
❖ *Place the pom poms blancs in a buttered baking pan. Brush each mushroom with butter and bake for 5 minutes.* ❖ *Remove from the oven, sprinkle with salt and pepper to taste and with the cress. Serve immediately.* ❖ Yield: 4 servings

To highlight the delicacy of the pom pom blanc, we nestle a fanciful serving plate on a bed of fresh leaves. Radish sprouts lend a contrasting crunch.

PLEUROTTE, OR OYSTER MUSHROOM

These mushrooms may be white, light gray, or light gray with a bluish tinge. They have small caps (about two inches wide) shaped like a fan, and come in clumps attached to a very short stem. Pleurottes are soft, silky, and fragrant, with a vague taste of shellfish. They are excellent sautéed, in casseroles, or cooked with fish or poultry. Pleurottes should not be washed, just wiped with a clean towel. The bottom of the stem must be trimmed. Separate the caps before cooking.

AVAILABILITY:
All year round, best in fall and winter.

SHOPPING GUIDE:
Select firm and fresh-looking mushrooms. Avoid shriveled and dry mushrooms.

STORAGE:
Will keep for 4 to 5 days, loosely wrapped in plastic, in the vegetable drawer of the refrigerator.

White oyster mushrooms, or pleurottes, are seen growing in their hothouse beds with all the drama of orchids.

An unusually large and dark oyster mushroom.

Pleurottes and Cinnamon Caps

◆ ◆ ◆

3 ounces cinnamon caps or nameko
mushrooms

¹/₄ pound pleurottes

4 tablespoons butter

Salt and pepper

1 tablespoon chopped fresh tarragon

3 cups fresh pea puree (see recipe, page 270)

Separate the mushroom caps from the stems, trim the stems, and set aside. In a skillet, melt the butter. Add the mushroom caps and stems and sauté for 5 minutes over medium heat. Season with salt and pepper to taste, add the tarragon, and cook for another 2 minutes. Remove from the heat.
❖ *Pour the fresh pea puree into a large bowl. Arrange the mushrooms on top and serve.* ❖
Yield: 4 servings

Resembling their namesake, oyster mushrooms
grow in large clusters. Malcolm Clark has a deft
hand at growing orchids, too.

PORCINO, BOLETE, OR CÈPE

This mushroom has a large, round, dark brown cap, measuring up to six inches in diameter, and pale, pungent, silken flesh. Porcini come from North America, Italy, and France. They are available fresh, frozen, and dried. They may be broiled, sautéed, stewed, or baked.

AVAILABILITY:
June to November.

SHOPPING GUIDE:
Select fresh-looking mushrooms with firm caps and unblemished stems. Avoid shriveled caps or dry-looking stems.

STORAGE:
Will keep for 2 to 3 days, loosely wrapped in plastic, in the vegetable drawer of the refrigerator. Best eaten as soon as possible.

Baked Stuffed Cèpes

◆ ◆ ◆

8 large cèpes (about 4 inches in diameter)

8 large shrimp, shelled and deveined

4 tablespoons butter

1 clove garlic, peeled and chopped

1 ½ cups breadcrumbs

4 tablespoons chopped fresh parsley

Salt and pepper

1 head Boston lettuce

Preheat the oven to 425 degrees.
❖ *Separate the mushroom caps from the stems, then wipe the caps with a clean cloth and set aside. Coarsely chop the stems. Place the shrimp in a saucepan, cover with boiling water, and bring to a boil over medium heat. Cook for 2 minutes and drain. Cool, then chop.* ❖ *In a skillet, melt 3 tablespoons of the butter. Add the chopped mushroom stems and the garlic and cook over medium heat, stirring occasionally, for 5 minutes. Add the breadcrumbs, parsley, and salt and pepper to taste. Cook for 2 minutes, stirring constantly. Remove from the heat.* ❖ *Fill the mushroom caps with the crumb mixture. Dot with remaining butter. Place the caps in a buttered 9 x 13-inch pan and bake for 30 minutes, or until the top is golden brown.* ❖ *Place a large lettuce leaf on each of 4 individual serving plates and top each with 2 stuffed mushrooms. Serve immediately.* ❖ Yield: 4 servings

The most versatile of all mushrooms, the porcino adds pungency to all manner of dishes, especially soups and poultry. ▶

Dried shiitake proffered for sale in New York's Chinatown. Once soaked to soften, dried shiitake can be used in soups, stews, and many braised dishes. The soaking liquid makes a heady base for vegetable bisques.

Just-picked shiitake are milder than dried and must be trimmed of stems before cooking.

SHIITAKE

This mushroom is cultivated in Asia, especially in China and Japan. In Chinese cuisine, shiitake mushrooms are mainly used dried; in Japanese cuisine, they are used fresh. The mushroom has a brownish-black cap two to four inches in diameter; it grows on oak logs in most parts of this country. Dried, the shiitake has a very intense flavor and aroma. (Dried shiitake must soak for at least one hour in lukewarm water.) Shiitake mushrooms can be sautéed, broiled, baked, used for stuffing poultry or fish, or mixed with noodles or rice. They give soups and vegetables a pungent aroma and rich taste. The stems are not good to eat.

AVAILABILITY:
All year round.

SHOPPING GUIDE:
Select shiitake mushrooms with firm, fresh caps. Avoid those with dry stems or mold on the caps.

STORAGE:
Will keep for 3 to 4 days, loosely wrapped in plastic, in the vegetable drawer of the refrigerator.

Consommé of Fresh and Dried Shiitake Mushrooms

◆ ◆ ◆

2 ounces dried shiitake mushrooms

$1/2$ pound fresh shiitake mushrooms

4 cups chicken broth

Salt and pepper

4 mint leaves

Cut off the stems of the dried shiitake and discard. Place the caps in a deep bowl and cover with lukewarm water. Soak for 1 hour. ❖ *Cut off the stems of the fresh shiitake and discard. Cut the caps in $1/8$ -inch strips and set aside.* ❖ *Drain the dried shiitake over a bowl and reserve the liquid.* ❖ *In a saucepan, heat the chicken broth. Add the dried shiitake. Bring to a boil, lower the heat, and simmer for 20 minutes. Using a slotted spoon, remove the dried shiitake, and save for another use. (They make an excellent stuffing for chicken.)* ❖ *Strain the shiitake soaking liquid and add to the broth. Add the fresh shiitake and cook over medium heat for 5 minutes. Correct the seasoning with salt and pepper to taste.* ❖ *Divide the soup among 4 serving bowls. Garnish with mint leaves and serve.* ❖ *Yield: 4 servings*

MOREL

Often imported from Europe, the morel, one of the most highly prized wild mushrooms, is also found in Michigan, Oregon, and Washington state, where it grows near aspens and in abandoned orchards. Morels resemble small sponges or honeycombs on hollow white stems; they have an earthy perfume. There are two types: the yellow morel, whose color varies from pale yellow to pale brown, and the black morel, which has a black cap. Either type is superb, whether sautéed simply or with scrambled eggs, stuffed, prepared in a cream sauce, or served with poached chicken or broiled beef.

Morels have to be washed thoroughly under cold running water, as the sponge-like caps often contain traces of earth. One easy way to clean the morel is to slice it in two lengthwise before washing. Cut off the base of the stem.

Dried morels are available year round. They must be soaked in several changes of warm water to remove any earth hidden in the honeycomb caps.

AVAILABILITY:
March to June.

SHOPPING GUIDE:
Select fresh, firm mushrooms.

STORAGE:
Best eaten the day they are bought.

Soft Scrambled Eggs with Morels

◆ ◆ ◆

6 tablespoons butter

½ pound morels, washed and coarsely chopped

8 eggs, lightly beaten

Salt and freshly ground pepper

In a skillet, melt 4 tablespoons of the butter over low heat. Add the morels and sauté for 3 minutes. Add the eggs and mix slowly over low heat with a wooden spoon. As the eggs cook, add the remaining butter in small pieces. The eggs should be soft. ❖ *Divide the scrambled eggs among 4 individual serving plates.* ❖ *Yield: 4 servings*

A playful arrangement of our favorite wild mushrooms. Clockwise from the upper right-hand corner: chanterelles, trompettes de la mort, white trompettes, shiitake, cinnamon caps, oyster mushrooms, and porcino.

GREEN LEAFY VEGETABLES

Despite my mother's coppery, feline eyes and her propensity for a meaty mushroom seared on the flame, despite her wooden spoons seen so often prodding a purple potato and her bamboo steamer hiding finger-sized lavender eggplants, my mother must eat several leaves each day to keep her sane—and tender toward me. As long as I can remember, she has served a green salad at the end of the evening meal, tossed with lemon juice, oil, salt, and pepper. We could tell when she had had a stressful day, or when fatigue clouded her spirit, simply by tasting this perfectly French, classically simple salad. Too tart, and we knew that we must tread softly; too salty, and we refrained from whining at the pile of dishes to be dried. But most of the time it was perfect: the leaves of mâche or escarole barely glossed, crisp, and buttery smooth, refreshed our palates and our minds for the dessert and homework ahead.

My mother's taste for leaves, however, goes beyond the green salad, something she thinks everyone should know how to make. She becomes a poetess in my eyes the moment flowering kale enters the realm of her imagination. Respecting its brilliant color and form, she pairs it with golden fish and the merest hint of garlic. Who else would create a flower whose petals are made from creamy white endive? And just the thought of her Swiss chard, tart, robust and fragrant, gives me a feeling of well-being.

Marianne is right! I cannot conceive of a meal without salad or at least a green leafy vegetable. I was quite bewildered when I came to New York from France thirty years ago. Salad was iceberg lettuce topped with a sweet, gloppy, orange-hued dressing that everyone called French—don't ask me why. It's not that I don't like iceberg: it reminds me of batavia, a French lettuce, tasteless

Flowering kale

Swiss chard

Sorrel

Broccoli raab

Watercress

Mesclun

Hydroponic lettuce

Radicchio

Dandelion

Mizuma

Mâche

◄ At the Farallones Institute in Santa Rosa, California, ruby-tinged kale grows abundantly among wildflower beds.

When picked at its peak of freshness, green kale has a delightfully piquant, grassy flavor, which we respect by keeping cooking time brief.

Totemic cones share planting space with buttery lettuces and herbs, protecting them from evil spirits and reminding visitors of the Farallones Institute's "commune" beginnings. ▶

but crunchy. I stuff its leaves with spicy minced chicken or clams or braise it with fresh herbs. I just don't use it as a salad. So for years, I searched—mostly in vain—for tender Boston lettuce, crunchy romaine, delicate frisée, buttery Bibb, and silken endive. I thought New York was never going to grow up!

Everything—my whole life!—changed with the advent of American nouvelle cuisine. A new generation of farmers, concerned about the environment, new types of produce, and more natural ways of farming cropped up (forgive the pun). We began to taste new fruits and vegetables from New Zealand, Australia, South America, and Africa. Fresh produce became the talk of the town as open markets sprung up in every major city. So I decided to meet some of the people who were improving the quality of my life.

Sonoma County, California, is the home of several important young organic farmers. My first stop was the Farallones Institute, outside of Santa Rosa, founded in the sixties by a group of hippies escaping the troubled and troubling city. Today, Farallones is run by an intense young man named Doug Gosling, with the help of three or four trainees. Part of this "certified organic" farm is a center for research and education; in the other part, Doug produces vegetables to feed the Institute's small community and also to sell at the local market and to restaurants in the San Francisco area. Farallones's beginnings still echo in its forms: the entrance to the garden—about five acres in a gently sloping valley—is protected by a goat skull, a totem pole tied with ribbons, and a bell, all representing the ancient spirits of the earth. Scattered almost randomly among the rows of mizuma (a Japanese feathery lettuce), perfect Russian red kale, small Chinese broccoli, mâche, and edible flowers are mystical cones, miniature spiritual houses, and little "monks" modeled in clay. Not far from a magnificent cardoon plant is a small copper church and, standing forlornly among the herbs, a statue of a heron with a necklace around his neck. The whole garden is peaceful, holy. I was moved.

John Carlson, manager of the garden of Santa Rosa Junior College, checks his beds of kale. His frisée salad is a hit at the local market.

Sorrel is one of Bob Cannard's prize crops in his Sonoma Valley garden. It is picked young to avoid bitterness.

The Sonoma Valley's occasional misty rains contribute to the lushness of Bob Cannard's farmland. Here, pickers are packing crates with sorrel. ▶

I continued my tour with a visit to John Carlson, the farm manager of the garden of Santa Rosa Junior College. John is forty-three years old, roly-poly, with a generous laugh. His garden has much charm. The yellow flowers of mustard plants danced in the breeze as John talked lovingly of his delicate frisée salad, long white leeks, bok choy, and garlic flowers. Most of what he grows is sold at the local market twice a week. As I was leaving, he bent down to pull a baby carrot from the ground, which he offered me with a flourish. The carrot was small, tender, and sweet.

There are other farmers in the area. Bob Cannard's garden was my next stop. He grows sorrel, tiny lettuces, fava beans, and Sugar Snap peas. Like many organic and experimental farmers in the Sonoma Valley, he relies on local distributing concerns to buy his vegetables.

Wineries have also become involved in growing produce. Many wineries in the Sonoma and Napa valleys invite the public to try the vegetables, salads, and fruit they grow along with their wines. The most beautiful garden belongs to Jim Fetzer of the Fetzer Vineyards. His love of vegetables and fruit prompted him, five years ago, to hire a young gardener, Michael Maltas, to establish a showcase garden. Michael is more traditional than the other organic farmers in the area in that he continues to grow those vegetables familiar to the winery's tourists, yet his garden is magnificent, as if drawn by an invisible hand. Not a weed mars the even rows: the colors are harmonious; the produce is perfect.

Today tender greens are available in specialty food stores, produce stands, and some supermarkets. Shopping for dinner now is not only a pleasure but an adventure. In the spring, I look for orache, a purple lettuce with tiny, rounded leaves, mâche, Bibb, and dandelion. In the summer, I find bittersweet sorrel, Swiss chard, baby leeks, and sprightly green onions.

The carefully laid out gardens of the Fetzer Vineyards display row upon row of luxurious salad greens, kale, and Swiss chard.

Dawn breaks over another part of the Fetzer gardens, where espaliered pear trees create green corridors in late summer.

This is just one of the many types of edible flowers now grown in the gardens and farms of the Sonoma Valley. ▶

On summer evenings, I serve a salad along with broiled steaks or cold chicken, and I often accompany a stew or other rich main course with a little mound of greens. I've also come up with several soups with a salad base, mostly when I gather the leftover leaves from the vegetable crisper after a week's worth of salads. The most successful of these is made with a chiffonnade of escarole poached in a strong chicken stock. I break a raw egg into the simmering broth and serve it straight away with grated parmesan cheese. My romaine soup is pureed first, then dotted with hot, crusty croutons and crumbled bacon. Marianne doesn't like my soups, complaining that they are plain and too often pureed. *Her* soups are different, she says. She patiently juliennes the salad leaves, allowing them to float in the broth. How unsatisfying, say I!

In early spring, the French enjoy mâche with sliced beets as an appetizer. Mâche, a tender, velvety, dark green salad recently made available in the United States, has become an important ingredient in many American chefs' repertoires. I've noticed, too, with glee, that the chef's salad of old has been reinterpreted. Instead of sliced egg, ham, and turkey on overly crisp greens, unusual salads are topped with duck confit, warm goat cheese, or shredded, marinated beef. The frisée with bacon and hot croutons that I enjoyed in my native France has become a staple of the American bistro menu. Vinaigrettes have also changed, and are composed of such tasty elements as raspberry and balsamic vinegars, walnut and extra-virgin olive oils. Salads are topped with thin slices of parmesan cheese, artichoke hearts, shiitake mushrooms, and sundried tomatoes. Relief is the word that comes to mind when I think of the recent revolution in salad-making . . . iceberg is now a taste of the past!

FLOWERING KALE, OR SALAD SAVOY

I came upon flowering kale in Scotland, where I was researching a story on smoked salmon. My contact there was a once-wealthy count, now impoverished, who had been left nothing but an ancestral castle and a passion for fishing. Logically, he had become a successful producer of smoked salmon. After a long and winding drive, I arrived at the castle gates. I remember his words of caution. "Once you're past the gates, please drive slowly, as I never know where my children are!" As I inched down the path toward the main house, I saw—instead of children— an extraordinary flower bed, in the midst of which were what seemed like cabbages. They had large ruffled green leaves and tightly curled centers that ranged from white to light pink to deep purple. After a tour of the smokehouse, I inquired about those strange "flowers." My host ex- plained that they were *Brassica oleracea*, the oldest member of the cabbage family. "No Victorian garden was without several flowering kale; it was used as an ornamen- tal plant," he said. Then he gave me a gleeful look. "My wife is preparing one for lunch."

The vegetable, like a giant rose, arrived cooked, on a silver platter, its shape and color intact. A lemony hollandaise was served alongside to soften its assertive, slightly bitter taste. A dish to delight the eye and satisfy the palate.

In the United States today, farmers are growing flowering kale for consump- tion as well as for the florists' windows. If you happen to have a potted flowering kale, you might consider cutting it and serving it to your guests.

AVAILABILITY:
October to December.

SHOPPING GUIDE:
Select full, medium heads (about the diameter of a dinner plate) with moist-looking, fresh leaves. Avoid wilted or brown leaves.

STORAGE:
A potted flowering kale can be kept in a cool, sunny spot for 1 to 2 weeks; water every 3 days. Will keep for about 3 days, wrapped in plastic, in the vegetable drawer of the refrigerator.

Ready to be cooked in a bamboo steamer, flowering kale is no less lovely than a real flower and comes in almost as many hues.

Steamed Flowering Kale with Veal in Ginger Sauce

◆ ◆ ◆

I pound leg of veal, thinly sliced

¼ cup flour

¼ cup vegetable oil

3 cloves garlic, peeled and chopped

Salt and pepper

I large flowering kale

2 scallions, thinly sliced

I ½ cups ginger sauce
(see recipe, page 268)

I tablespoon olive oil

Preheat the oven to 200 degrees.
❖ *Cut the veal into thin strips, about ⅛ x 2 inches. Twist each strip and bring the ends together to form a circle. Attach the ends together with a toothpick and dust lightly with flour.* ❖ *In a skillet, heat the oil. When the oil is hot, add the garlic, sauté until golden, then add the veal strips and sauté briefly, turning once, until golden brown. Using a slotted spoon, transfer veal to a plate. Sprinkle with salt and pepper and keep warm in the oven.* ❖ *Steam the kale, whole, for 10 minutes, or until tender.* ❖ *Place the kale on a large platter. Sprinkle with salt and pepper.* ❖ *Using kitchen shears, cut several leaves off at the stem and arrange 5 or 6 of them on each of 4 individual serving plates to resemble the petals of a flower. Remove the toothpicks and arrange the veal in the center of each plate. Sprinkle with the sliced scallions and serve promptly, with the ginger sauce alongside.* ❖ *Drizzle the remaining leaves with olive oil and serve with the meal.* ❖
Yield: 4 servings

Flowering kale leaves, arranged to resemble petals, are the perfect foil for sautéed veal. We added radish sprouts, olives, and rosemary.

SWISS AND RUBY CHARD

I can't bear beets but I love bettes. *The leaves of a particular type of beet,* bette, *known as Swiss chard in the United States, are a spinach-like vegetable that (above the root) has two distinct parts: the rib and the green leaf. When I was growing up, my mother would buy Swiss chard (being French, she never learned to pronounce the* d, *so until recently I thought it was spelled* char), *cut away the stiff, white ribs, and cooked the leaves as she would spinach. All well and good; I enjoyed, and even preferred, chard's mild flavor to spinach's astringent bite. When I went to France to live, however, I discovered that the ribs were even more highly prized than the leaves. As a matter of fact, the leaves are often referred to as* les restes, *or leftovers. In the south of France, the ribs are cooked for about half an hour in a broth flavored with a bouquet garni and an onion, then drained and sautéed in olive oil with garlic and parsley. The "leftovers" are often finely chopped and used to stuff a sweet pastry, along with pine nuts, raisins, brandy, and sugar. In Paris, where I lived, the ribs are prepared in broth as in the south, but allowed to cool; then they are served with mayonnaise, in the manner of asparagus, or gratinéed in a béchamel sauce.*

Now that I'm a Yankee again, I have come to a culinary compromise, respecting the ribs and the leaves equally, and using more and more often the beautiful ruby chard, which has scarlet stems and deep green, velvety leaves. My mother still says "char," I say "bettes," and we serve the vegetable in myriad ways—in a luscious flan and stuffed with spicy chicken, among others—from the beginning of spring through the early months of fall.

A single leaf of Swiss chard and one of ruby chard.

AVAILABILITY:
All year round; best in summer.

SHOPPING GUIDE:
Select bunches with bright green leaves and crisp stems.

STORAGE:
Will keep for about 2 days, wrapped in plastic, in the vegetable drawer of the refrigerator.

Chicken Breasts Stuffed with Swiss Chard

❖ ❖ ❖

2 whole boneless chicken breasts, cut in half

Salt and pepper

Juice of ½ lemon

1 pound Swiss chard

1 teaspoon minced fresh thyme leaves

1 clove garlic, peeled and minced

1 cup chicken broth

2 tablespoons olive oil

Paprika

Preheat oven to 350 degrees.
❖ *Flatten the chicken breasts between pieces of wax paper, using the back of skillet to pound on the breasts. Sprinkle with salt and pepper and marinate for 15 minutes in lemon juice.* ❖ *Wash and trim the Swiss chard. Bring 2 quarts of water to a boil and blanch the chard for 5 minutes. Drain and refresh under cold water. Squeeze the water out with your hands. Coarsely chop the chard leaves and stems. Add salt and pepper to taste and the minced thyme and garlic. Mix well.* ❖ *Divide the chard in 4 parts. Place one part in each chicken breast, fold the sides under, and secure with toothpicks.* ❖ *Place the chicken breasts, seam side down, in a 9 x 12-inch baking pan. Pour the broth into the pan. Brush the chicken breasts with the oil and bake for 25 minutes, or until golden brown.* ❖ *Arrange the chicken breasts on 4 individual serving plates, sprinkle with paprika, and serve with the pan juices.* ❖ *Yield: 4 servings*

Chard leaves grow together in clumps like the one pictured; chard is sold, however, in bunches of loose leaves.

SORREL

Edith is a wonder. She is my mother's closest friend and my "second mother," and she grows sorrel in her Massachusetts garden. Lots of sorrel. She likes to laugh and she gives away her sorrel by the bagful. Edith's generosity leads me, every spring, to make soupe à l'oseille, *the simple, classic green velouté served during the mild months in France.*

Describing the taste of sorrel is a writer's ultimate challenge. The curled, soft green leaves, much like spinach leaves, are acrid and bitter when mature and raw. It's not surprising to find out that the plant is related to rhubarb, another of Edith's bumper crops. But when sorrel is stewed in a bit of butter or drop of water, it mellows and sweetens, just enough to echo the flavor and scents of a meadow. It is a mystery to me that American farmers and gardeners have, for so long, neglected this fragrant leaf—one that has flavored the stews and soups of Central and Eastern Europe for at least eight centuries.

When picked young, sorrel leaves can be added raw to salads for a lemony taste or chopped over fish. But there is nothing better than a light, smooth sorrel soup. Edith prepares hers with neither butter nor cream, so that the true nature of the plant comes through. She adds a touch of horseradish for added piquancy, and a dollop of yogurt for contrast. I tend not to stray so far from the traditional: I "melt" the chopped leaves in a bit of sweet butter, then add enough stock to liquefy. Cream, I feel, cuts the grassy taste; salt and pepper intensify the lemony undertones. It is my favorite soup.

As much as I love sorrel soup, I wrinkle my nose at saumon à l'oseille *and other sundry preparations with sorrel sauce served in France and in French restaurants in America. Sorrel sauce found its way onto so many fish fillets that, at least for me, the novelty wore off. On the other hand, I enjoy the sauce atop certain steamed vegetables that might need a boost of flavor or color, such as chayote or spaghetti squash. I also occasionally sprinkle a few shreds into an omelet and use it, too, as an herb in marinades.*

AVAILABILITY:
April to July.

SHOPPING GUIDE:
Select bunches with bright green, young leaves. Avoid yellow leaves or tough, stringy stems, which indicate maturity. Allow at least 3 ounces per person (for soup): sorrel reduces a great deal when cooked.

STORAGE:
Will keep for 3 to 4 days, wrapped in plastic, in the vegetable drawer of the refrigerator.

◄ Sorrel flowers, although very pretty, indicate mature plants. We like our sorrel picked extra young and sweet, especially for soups.

John Gorzynski proudly shows off his young sorrel crop, which he will cart to New York's Green-market from his farm in upstate Cochecton Center.

Shoots of wild sorrel. An annual, wild sorrel, with its small leaves and delicate stems, is more bitter than its cultivated cousin and needs a touch of sugar to be palatable.

Edith's Sorrel Soup

♦ ♦ ♦

3 pounds sorrel

1 tablespoon oil

2 shallots, peeled and chopped

2 medium potatoes, peeled and cubed

6 cups chicken broth

Salt and pepper

1 tablespoon prepared horseradish

½ cup plain yogurt

Wash and drain the sorrel. Trim off the thick stems. In a saucepan, heat the oil, add the shallots, and sauté over medium heat until transparent. Add the sorrel and cook, stirring, until wilted. ❖ *Add the potatoes and the broth. Bring to a boil, lower the heat, and simmer for 20 minutes. Remove from the heat and transfer to the bowl of a food processor. Process until smooth. Pour back into the saucepan, add salt and pepper to taste, and add the horseradish. Mix well and gently reheat.* ❖ *Divide the soup among 4 serving bowls, garnish each with a dollop of yogurt, and serve.* ❖ Yield: 4 servings

We chose to garnish Edith's sorrel soup with a handful of Royal Ann cherries, as a reminder that both herald the spring. Radish sprouts give color to the dollop of yogurt.

BROCCOLI RAAB

I knew I was growing up when I first tasted broccoli raab. I was about eleven then, and had a particular fondness for broccoli, which my mother steamed until tender and sprinkled with coarse salt. It was like eating whole trees that were sweet and fresh-tasting. We had just moved into a new house and the children were often sent alone (with the family dog) to a neighborhood Italian restaurant, where we dined on stuffed artichokes and lasagne. One night, my sister dared to order veal, and it came with a side dish of broccoli raab, soaking in olive oil, white wine, and garlic. She promptly offered it to our dog (he would eat anything), but I rescued the plate and ate it all. Its bitterness and complexity took me by surprise, but I was ready for it. The family dog never forgave me. Now that I am truly grown up, I like to serve it braised with the Italian grain spelt *and tiny, homemade veal meatballs.*

*You may find broccoli raab under many different names—broccoli rabe, brocoletti di rape, rappini, choy sum, gai lan—in produce stores, Chinese markets, and, recently, in supermarkets. Related to the turnip (*rapa *means turnip in Italian), broccoli raab has no true "head" but rather small buds and tiny yellow flowers at the blossom end of long stalks. Its green leaves are pungent and slightly bitter. European broccoli raab has shorter, thinner stalks and smaller flower buds than the Chinese variety. My mother prefers the Chinese variety, which she claims is sweeter and does not require blanching (see page 134).*

I often do my food shopping in Manhattan's Chinatown. For years, I've passed an old woman selling Chinese dried foods from a wooden cart on Canal Street. Not ordinary things like jasmine tea but dried mussels, snake skins, tree bark, petrified ginger, and all sorts of dried mushrooms. One day, I saw that she was peddling something that looked like feathery white coral. With rather wild gesturing and the help of a customer who happened to speak some English, I learned that it was seaweed. "Delicious," claimed the customer. "Soak in water, very good for..." she said as she pointed to her stomach. I bought a half pound (about ten "balls") and dropped them in a bowl of lukewarm water as soon as I got home. Twenty minutes later, I thought a mysterious creature from outer space had entered my kitchen and was about to swallow me up. Each ball had doubled, no, tripled, in size, and they were overflowing the bowl. But I was brave. I shook them dry, cut them up, and sautéed them with broccoli raab. They were sweet and crunchy, with a faint aftertaste of the sea. I thought of a tabloid headline: WOMAN EATS CREATURE FROM MARS AND LIVES. Actually, I thrived.

AVAILABILITY:
November to March.

SHOPPING GUIDE:
Select bunches with crisp leaves, firm stalks, and moist, green stem ends. Avoid split stalks, wilting leaves, and overly bloomed heads.

STORAGE:
Will keep for up to 5 days, wrapped in plastic, in the vegetable drawer of the refrigerator.

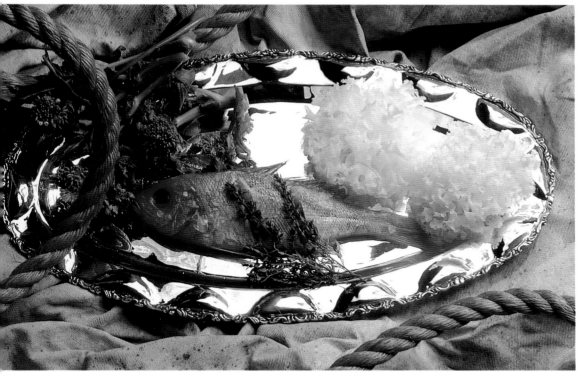

Broccoli raab's slight bitterness enlivens a red snapper, shown ready to be broiled with thyme and garnished with Chinese white seaweed balls.

Red Snapper with Broccoli Raab

◆ ◆ ◆

4 small red snappers
(about I pound each)

4 sprigs fresh thyme

2 tablespoons olive oil

½ pound dried white seaweed
(about 10 balls) soaked in lukewarm
water for 30 minutes

Salt and pepper

1 ½ pounds broccoli raab

2 tablespoons vegetable oil

½ tablespoon sesame oil

2 cloves garlic, peeled and sliced

1 tablespoon sugar

1 lemon, quartered

Preheat the broiler.
❖ *Wash and pat dry the fish. Place 1 sprig of thyme inside each one. Brush with olive oil and set aside.* ❖ *Drain and quarter the seaweed balls and set aside. In a large saucepan, bring to a boil 2 quarts of water with 1 teaspoon salt. Add the broccoli raab, cook for 5 minutes, drain, and set aside.* ❖ *In the same saucepan, heat the oils. Add the garlic and sauté for 1 minute. Add the broccoli, white seaweed, and sugar. Mix well. Cook over low heat for 5 minutes. Correct the seasoning and keep warm.* ❖ *Sprinkle the fish with salt and pepper. Broil for about 4 to 5 minutes on each side.* ❖ *Place a fish on each of 4 individual serving plates. Arrange the broccoli raab and seaweed around the fish. Garnish with a lemon wedge and serve.* ❖ *Yield: 4 servings*

◄ A bunch of fresh broccoli raab. Unlike conventional broccoli, its stems, leaves, and budding heads do not require separate cooking times. Braised broccoli raab is an Italian classic.

WATERCRESS

Watercress, with its small, dark green leaves, long stems, and mustardy bite, is as common today as iceberg lettuce was twenty years ago. I often wonder what restaurants would do if watercress went on strike. How would they garnish their plates?

Watercress wasn't always so popular, though. Many years ago, I created and hosted a television series on cooking for children. One of the segments was to be filmed in a Southern town. I had chosen to teach the little children on the show how to make a watercress soup. Little did I know that watercress was not sold in stores. The day of the shooting came and, to my dismay, I was told by the director that his crew could not find watercress anywhere in town. Desperate, I decided to go on the radio and appeal directly to the townspeople. I described watercress, explained that it grew on the banks of small brooks, that it tasted slightly piquant, and that anyone with a brook should go and look for watercress, pick some, and bring it to the studio. Within an hour, I had truckloads of watercress at my feet!

Watercress shouldn't just be considered for garnish or even soup. It is wonderful mixed with Belgian endive or green leaf lettuce; steamed and sautéed with garlic and olive or sesame oil; stuffed into pita bread with a hamburger, or processed with bean curd into a light sauce for cold roasts.

Watercress is sold in bunches of about ½ pound. When using it as a salad, discard the stems. When cooking watercress, remember that it reduces by half.

AVAILABILITY:
All year round.

SHOPPING GUIDE:
Select bunches with dark green leaves and firm stems.

STORAGE:
Will keep for 2 days, wrapped in plastic, in the vegetable drawer of the refrigerator.

Watercress Soufflé in a Grapefruit

◆ ◆ ◆

2 grapefruit

2 pounds watercress, trimmed (4 bunches)

3 tablespoons butter

Salt and freshly ground pepper

3 egg yolks

4 egg whites

Preheat the oven to 375 degrees.
❖ *Cut each grapefruit in half. With a grapefruit knife, remove the flesh (it can be squeezed later for juice), being careful not to tear the skin. Set aside.* ❖ *Wash, drain, and pat dry the watercress with paper towels. Cut off the larger stems.* ❖ *In a saucepan, melt the butter. Add the watercress and cook, stirring, for a few minutes, or until it wilts. Sprinkle with salt and pepper to taste. Mix well and remove from the heat.* ❖ *Place the watercress and egg yolks in the bowl of a food processor and process until the mixture is pureed.* ❖ *In a bowl, beat the egg whites with a pinch of salt until stiff. Gently fold the watercress mixture into the egg whites.* ❖ *Fill the 4 grapefruit halves with the watercress mixture. Bake for 20 minutes or until a cake tester inserted in the center comes out clean.* ❖ *Serve immediately.*
❖ *Yield: 4 servings*

MESCLUN

My son once said that the word mesclun sounded more like a war than a salad (he must have been thinking of Verdun). He was right in that mesclun is not a single salad, but a mixture of young, tender leaves from many different salads. In the Paris open markets, mounds of mesclun always attracted me. Like a painter's dream, the colors of mesclun range from spring green to buttery yellow to delicate brush strokes of red and white. Today, mesclun is available in most produce markets and in some supermarkets in the United States. It makes a glorious, sunny ending to any meal.

AVAILABILITY:
All year round.

SHOPPING GUIDE:
Select small, crisp, fresh-looking leaves.

STORAGE:
Will keep for 1 week, wrapped in plastic, in the vegetable drawer of the refrigerator.

Salad of Mesclun with Daisies

◆ ◆ ◆

½ pound mesclun

½ cup lemon vinaigrette
(see recipe, page 269)

1 ounce edible daisies or any other
edible flowers

4 hot French rolls

Butter

Place the salad in a bowl, add the vinaigrette, and toss lightly. ❖ *Divide the salad among 4 salad plates and garnish with the daisies. Serve with rolls and butter.* ❖ *Yield: 4 servings*

◀ Mesclun, a mixture of small lettuce leaves of various types, is the quintessential image of freshness. Here, we've tossed in a handful of edible flowers to create a meadow ready to eat.

HYDROPONIC LETTUCE

Hydroponic lettuce was created in Louisiana, where tender lettuce leaves were becoming very popular when Marianne and I began to do research on salads. The lettuce is grown in troughs filled with water. When harvested, the entire head with the stem and a small clump of earth still attached is packed in a plastic box that encloses the lettuce without bruising the leaves. Hydroponic lettuce is always perfect. Its leaves are buttery soft, pale green, and as tasty as a garden-grown Boston lettuce. Marianne and I like to stuff individual leaves with leftover ground pot roast or turkey.

AVAILABILITY:
All year round.

SHOPPING GUIDE:
Select heads with crisp, bright green leaves. Avoid bruised or wilted leaves and a dried-out stem.

STORAGE:
Will keep 2 to 3 days in its unopened plastic box in the refrigerator.

Lettuce Stuffed with Pot Roast

◆ ◆ ◆

4 heads hydroponic lettuce

2 cups chopped leftover pot roast or cooked chopped veal

1 tablespoon minced fresh thyme

1 egg

1/2 cup leftover sauce from roast or 1/2 cup beef broth

Salt and pepper

1 tablespoon olive oil

2 cups red pepper sauce
(see recipe, page 270)

Cut off the stems of the lettuce. Carefully spread apart the center leaves and remove the heart. Coarsely chop it and set it aside. ❖ *In a bowl, combine the chopped pot roast, thyme, egg, chopped lettuce, and leftover sauce and mix well. Taste and correct the seasoning. Fill the lettuce cavities and press the leaves together to enclose the stuffing. Sprinkle with salt and pepper and brush with olive oil.* ❖ *Place the 4 stuffed heads of lettuce in a steamer and steam for 4 minutes. If using a metal steamer, line with lettuce leaves.* ❖ *Carefully remove the lettuces with a spatula and place on 4 individual serving plates. Pour some red pepper sauce around the lettuce and serve.* ❖ Yield: 4 servings

A sprinkling of chopped pistachios and an edible flower garnish this stuffed head of hydroponic lettuce. This dish makes a spectacular main course, yet is easy to prepare. ▶

RADICCHIO

Walking down the produce aisles, I often get ideas for dishes I would like to cook. When I am in one of my avant-garde moods, I dream up rather strange combinations of ingredients; sometimes these creations turn out to be delicious, sometimes dreadful. More often than not, they do not visually resemble what I had imagined. This is what happened to me when I first cooked radicchio. In my mind's eye, I saw the brilliant purple-red of cooked radicchio surrounding the orange-pink of poached salmon, just like a Caribbean sunset. The end result was a dun-colored blob, tasty but with none of the brilliance of my dream.

Anyway, radicchio is delectable when sautéed with fresh herbs, or used as a topping for fresh pasta or steamed baby summer squash. I'll never stop dreaming.

The Italians export two kinds of radicchio to the United States. One, called *radicchio rosso* or *radicchio di Verona,* is round, with loosely overlapping deep red leaves. *Radicchio di Treviso* has long, narrow red leaves with white ribs attached at the base around a brown root. The radicchio grown here has tightly overlapping leaves and tends to be slightly bitter. All three are delicious eaten raw in salads or cooked.

AVAILABILITY:
All year round.

SHOPPING GUIDE:
Select firm and crisp heads with shiny leaves. Avoid brown spots, leaves shriveled at the edges, and dried stem ends.

STORAGE:
Will keep for 2 to 3 days, wrapped in plastic, in the vegetable drawer of the refrigerator.

A head of *radicchio di Treviso* ready to be picked. These dark scarlet leaves are tender and less bitter than the more common *radicchio rosso*.

Braised radicchio is cooked in just a modicum of butter and flavored with fresh basil.

Braised Radicchio

• • •

2 pounds radicchio

3 tablespoons butter

Salt and pepper

$^1/_2$ cup chopped fresh basil

Quarter each radicchio head, then cut each quarter into 2-inch pieces, separating the leaves. ❖ *In a saucepan, melt the butter over medium heat. When the butter is hot, add the radicchio and cook, stirring constantly, until wilted. Season with salt and pepper to taste. Remove from the heat.* ❖ *Place the radicchio in a serving dish, sprinkle with chopped basil, and serve.* ❖ Yield: 4 servings

....

DANDELION

One of my earliest memories of my father is of him walking through the fields with me—just a toddler then, a basket dangling on my arm—holding my hand very tightly as we went looking for dandelion greens. My father would stop suddenly when he spied a cluster of jagged leaves jolting upward from the ground. He would pick them and throw them in my basket, and when it was full, we would walk back to the house, my father smacking his lips in anticipation. In the kitchen, he would cut cubes of streaky slab bacon and brown them. Then cubes of bread would be tossed into the skillet and fried until golden. Both topped a pile of dewy dandelion greens. He'd mix rich wine vinegar with olive oil and add a spoonful of hot bacon fat. We'd sit down to eat the salad, slightly bitter yet mellow, alone. Just my father and me.

Dandelions can be steamed, sautéed, braised, and pureed for soup. In the United States, dandelions grow in fields and lawns, to the dismay of gardeners and the delight of knowing cooks. They are sometimes sold in farmers markets during the spring and summer. What's sold in gourmet produce stores is cultivated.

AVAILABILITY:
Early spring to late summer.

SHOPPING GUIDE:
Select small, crisp leaves, the younger the better. Avoid leaves with brown or shriveled edges.

STORAGE:
Will keep for 4 to 5 days, wrapped in plastic, in the vegetable drawer of the refrigerator.

◄ Freshly picked wild flowering dandelion greens are used in the traditional French salad *pissenlit,* in which they are tossed with a warm vinaigrette and chopped bacon.

Steamed Dandelions with Beets

• • •

¾ pound fresh beets, cooked and peeled, or 1 16-ounce can whole beets, drained

2 pounds dandelions

2 tablespoons olive oil

1 tablespoon red wine vinegar

1 clove garlic, minced

Salt and pepper

2 lemons, thinly sliced

4 hard-boiled eggs, peeled and sliced

Slice the beets and set aside. ❖ *Wash and trim off 1 inch at the root end of each bunch of dandelions. Dandelion clumps sometimes have tiny flowers: if they are organic, you may cook them; if not, discard the flowers. In a saucepan, bring 2 quarts of water to a boil. Add 1 teaspoon salt and the dandelions. Bring back to a boil and turn off the heat. Let the dandelions soak in the water for several minutes, then drain and refresh under cold water. Drain again and pat dry with paper towels.* ❖ *In a bowl, combine the oil, vinegar, garlic, and salt and pepper to taste.* ❖ *Arrange the dandelion greens on a serving platter and decorate with a line of sliced beets alternating with slices of lemon and egg. Pour some dressing over the dandelion and serve.* Yield: 4 servings

MIZUMA

It was while visiting some of California's innovative young farmers that I first tasted mizuma. A vegetable imported by Japanese farmers, mizuma has a delicate, feathery texture that, when coupled with romaine or other common lettuces, adds a touch of lightness. Mizuma is not yet available in supermarkets but can be found during the spring and summer months in many farmers markets and gourmet produce stores.

Mizuma should be quickly washed, then thoroughly dried before using. It is a good replacement for frisée, the pale yellow French salad green. I also like to use it as I would watercress in tea sandwiches.

Cooked mizuma is excellent, but you need a lot of it to make a vegetable dish, since it reduces by half when cooked.

AVAILABILITY:
Early spring to late summer.

SHOPPING GUIDE:
Select fresh, crisp leaves. Avoid those with slightly discolored ones.

STORAGE:
Will keep 4 to 5 days, wrapped in plastic, in the vegetable drawer of the refrigerator.

Mizuma Tea Sandwiches

• • •

1 loaf white bread, thinly sliced

½ pound mizuma

¼ pound smoked salmon

1 8-ounce package cream cheese

Trim the crusts from each slice of bread. ❖ *Wash the mizuma and pat dry with paper towels. Coarsely chop the smoked salmon; place in a bowl with the cream cheese and mix well with a fork.* ❖ *Spread the cream cheese mixture on half the bread slices. Top with mizuma leaves and cover with a slice of bread. Cut each sandwich diagonally and stack, pyramid-fashion, on a serving platter.* ❖ *Cover the platter with a damp kitchen towel or seal with plastic wrap until ready to serve.* ❖ Yield: 30 tea sandwiches

Originally from Japan, mizuma, pictured here growing at the Farallones Institute, is a feathery, tender, and sweet green leaf that lends itself to salad mixtures such as mesclun. ▶

MÂCHE

Parisians know when spring has arrived with the advent of piles of mâche in open-air markets and with its appearance on restaurant menus. Its dark green, small, velvety leaves form little clusters with thread-like roots that must be removed before the salad is washed. When I complained to a Canadian friend that mâche was not available in the United States, she sent me a packet of seeds labeled lamb's lettuce. Once I planted them, I realized that lamb's lettuce was simply an English name for my beloved mâche. Mâche is a salad green that is too delicate to withstand the heat of cooking. It can be tossed with a vinaigrette, alone or in combination with sliced Belgian endive, sliced beets, or hard-boiled eggs, or served as a garnish for steak or roast chicken.

Today, mâche is imported from France and Holland and grown in the United States as well, although the latter is not quite as lush as its European brothers. Both kinds are available in gourmet produce stores.

AVAILABILITY:
All year round.

SHOPPING GUIDE:
Select clusters with bright, fresh-looking leaves. Avoid limp, thin clusters.

STORAGE:
Will keep 2 to 3 days, wrapped loosely in plastic, in the refrigerator.

The leaves of mâche, or corn salad, are very small—about the size of a pinky tip—and velvety. A harbinger of spring, mâche is particularly sweet and rich.

ROOTS

As autumn's rain falls and the wind sweeps up golden leaves so that they stick to the window panes, my mother and I drink tea together. And in our minds, we dig down into the moist soil of a vegetable garden and pull up dark and gnarly roots that smell of earth. Salsify and turnips, celeriac and rutabaga, jícama and Jerusalem artichokes . . . we share a taste for them that goes beyond the heavy soups of yesteryear, in which they played so dominant a part. Although some claim that roots are bland, we have come to appreciate their enigmatic, adaptable, and delicate flavors. After the warmth of tea and mother-daughter conversation, we take up our sharp little knives and peel away until we discover the best way to transform roots into rhapsodies from the kitchen.

Most of the root vegetables that interest us are—unlike their underground cousins, the tubers—delicious in the raw. We sprinkle coarse salt onto white disks of turnip (we like these with the snap of icy aquavit) or toss raw grated jícama with chopped watercress and a vinaigrette made with dry English mustard. Some roots must be cooked but, for us, that doesn't mean tossing them into a pot where a chicken is bubbling. We like to shock, so we pair glazed tangerines with burdock and toss sundried tomatoes into a celeriac soup.

We have our personal favorites, too. Colette loves kohlrabi. On my last birthday, she surprised me with a dessert of sweetened kohlrabi puree served in ripe persimmons. And I love parsnips. One Indian summer day, when the heat just wiped Colette out, I brought her an ice-cold gin and tonic and a plate of cold shredded parsnips tossed with lime and salt.

I guess you could say that our roots are right at our fingertips and attached to our hearts.

Burdock

Celeriac

Kohlrabi

Jícama

Turnip

Jerusalem artichoke

Rutabaga

Parsley root

Parsnip

◄ A crate of burdock. The Japanese version of salsify, burdock is an elongated root; the pinkish tops (the leaves are cut before being brought to market) pop out of the ground.

BURDOCK

During one of my trips to Japan, I traveled north to Wajima to visit a nun named Seitouchi, whom I'd met in New York. Seitouchi, who delighted in my love of Japanese food, arranged for me to be entertained by a farmer whose wife was said to be an excellent cook. As we sat around the brazier in the center of the house, the farmer's wife served us hot sake in wooden cups and an appetizer made from fish paste wrapped around a slightly crunchy, sweet vegetable with the taste of artichoke. Seitouchi responded to my inquisitive look by drawing what looked like a salsify on a piece of scrap paper. She called it burdock in English.

To complete my education, Seitouchi took me to an open-air market the next morning. There, she pointed to bunches of whole burdock. The long, narrow "sticks," about the thickness of a carrot, resembled salsify but were rust-colored, not black or white. When I returned home, I found that burdock is grown in California and Hawaii and is available in many health-food stores and Japanese markets. If I can't get hold of burdock, I simply substitute salsify, which has a very similar taste and holds its shape better when cooked.

Burdock and salsify can be pureed, added to soups, used in tempura, braised with mushrooms, prepared *au gratin*, and tossed in seafood salads. As soon as the vegetable is peeled, drop it into a bowl of acidulated water; it quickly turns brown upon contact with the air.

I thank the gods my mother thinks she's Japanese. Before she was "reborn," I placed salsify low on the vegetable ladder, finding it fibrous, woody, bland, and altogether unappealing. Now that she's taken several trips to her new "home" in the Orient, I've learned to appreciate salsify, scorzonera (black salsify), and, of course, the elongated Japanese burdock. Its musty taste—why some liken it to the oyster, *I'll never know—flavors sauces as the mushroom does, with earthiness and smoke. If cooked correctly, burdock is tender to the bite without being mushy. The secret is soaking the peeled vegetable in acidulated water for about ten minutes; this rids it of any bitterness.*

And so, my mother dons her wooden platform thongs, wields a sharp kitchen cleaver bought in Hong Kong, and fills her counter with bottles of dashi *(Japanese fish stock) and soy sauce. Very grateful, I eat her burdock and refrain from teasing her.*

AVAILABILITY:
All year round; best in winter.

SHOPPING GUIDE:
Select roots that look young and are earth stained, if possible. Avoid limpness.

STORAGE:
Will keep for 5 to 6 days, wrapped in a damp cloth, in the vegetable drawer of the refrigerator.

A bamboo basket is filled with tiny onions, taro, and burdock. A sprig of fresh bay leaves completes this centerpiece.

Chicken Breasts with Burdock

❖   ❖   ❖

2 pounds burdock or salsify, peeled and cut
into 3-inch pieces

I lemon

Salt and pepper

2 tablespoons butter

6 scallions

2 pounds boneless chicken breasts, thinly sliced

I tablespoon chopped fresh parsley

2 cloves garlic, peeled and minced

¼ cup soy sauce

I tablespoon sesame oil

Parsley sprigs for garnish

I cup red pepper sauce
(see recipe, page 270)

Soak the burdock in cold water with the juice of half the lemon for 10 minutes.   ❖   *Drain the burdock and place in a large saucepan. Cover with water and add the remaining lemon half (rind and all) and ³/₄ teaspoon salt. Bring to a boil, lower the heat to medium, and cook for 15 to 20 minutes, or until tender. Drain.*   ❖   *In a saucepan, heat the butter, add the burdock, sprinkle with salt and pepper, and sauté for 3 minutes. Remove from the heat and cool.*   ❖   *Trim the scallions and cut in quarters lengthwise.*   ❖   *Preheat the broiler.*   ❖   *Place a slice of chicken breast on a serving plate. Sprinkle with salt and pepper, ¼ teaspoon of the chopped parsley, and a pinch of garlic. Place a piece of burdock in the center and arrange a piece of scallion, the green part sticking out, next to the burdock. Roll the chicken breast tightly around the burdock and secure with a toothpick. Set aside. Continue for the remaining slices of chicken.*   ❖   *Combine the soy sauce and sesame oil. Brush the chicken with this mixture. Broil under a very hot broiler for 4 minutes on each side.*   ❖   *Place the chicken rolls on a platter and garnish with parsley sprigs. Heat the remaining burdock and serve alongside the chicken. Serve the red pepper sauce in a sauceboat.*   ❖   *Yield: 4 servings*

Burdock and scallions are tucked into rolls of chicken breast. A red pepper sauce, served in a tangerine shell, adds dimension to the broiled chicken. A fricassee of chanterelles makes this simple dish elegant.

Burdock with Red Peppers

• • •

2 pounds burdock or salsify, peeled and cut
into 2-inch pieces

Juice of ½ lemon

4 cups chicken broth

2 red peppers

Two 3 ½ -ounce packages enoki mushrooms

2 tablespoons vegetable oil

1 clove garlic, peeled and crushed

1 tablespoon soy sauce

¼ tablespoon sesame oil

5 Chinese or garlic chives, chopped

*Soak the burdock in cold water with the lemon
juice for 10 minutes. Drain.* ❖ *Boil the burdock
in the chicken broth for 15 minutes, or until tender. Drain.* ❖ *Cut the red peppers lengthwise
into 2-inch slices. Remove the seeds. Trim the
enoki mushrooms.* ❖ *In a wok, heat the oil with
the garlic. Add the burdock and the peppers and
sauté until the red pepper is cooked, about 5
minutes. Add the soy sauce, sesame oil, and
mushrooms. Sauté for 1 more minute. Remove
from the heat.* ❖ *Sprinkle with the chives, and
arrange on serving platter.* ❖ Yield: 4 servings

About to be stir-fried, pieces of burdock share
wok space with red bell pepper and enoki
mushrooms.

CELERIAC, OR CELERY ROOT

There are a few days in the fall when my husband and I look at each other and sigh knowingly. The wind is moist and cool, the sky overcast, the air just warm enough to allow thick sweaters without an overcoat. We sigh because, on those particular fall days, we miss the French countryside, where we used to hunt small game in the morning and eat a prodigious meal at midday, prepared by my deft, if cantankerous, mother-in-law. On those fall days, we call France, speak to la famille, *and make rabbit stew for supper. The evening meal begins with* céleri rémoulade, *the classic French fall salad of shredded celeriac tossed with a mustard mayonnaise. Mine has never matched my mother-in-law's in mellowness, but my husband insists it chases away his twinge of homesickness.*

I prefer celeriac to celery. An emotional reaction, as I associate celery with tuna salad and Liptauer cheese, two foods I've never been able to stomach. Celeriac, with its untamed, sweet, and honest flavor, is a boon for dieters (it's low in calories), but I love it for its prehistoric appearance and its versatility. And, of course, for the memories it engenders.

Celeriac has also served as a bridge between me and the husband of my closest friend. Carl, a handsome young architect-turned-caterer, is from Stuttgart, Germany, and when I first met him, he was a bit reserved. Dinner, which he whipped up in no time, consisted of expertly grilled salmon steaks and a vegetable puree. Pressed to tell us what it was made from, he made a guessing game out of the mystery. We failed miserably, not able to discern the subtle flavors of celeriac, apple, and the merest hint of lemon. This guessing game became a tradition and Carl warmed up to me, revealing himself as a charming person and a wizard in the kitchen. He even shared his recipe with me. It consists of pureeing three pounds of

peeled and cooked celeriac with one peeled and cooked Granny Smith apple, the zest of half a lemon, a third of a cup of cream, a pinch of nutmeg, and salt and pepper to taste. I have since served Carl's celeriac puree at countless dinner parties.

AVAILABILITY:
September to April; best in fall.

SHOPPING GUIDE:
Select smaller roots (up to 1 pound). Avoid those with cracks or sponginess at the stalk end.

STORAGE:
Will keep for 6 to 10 days, wrapped in plastic, in the vegetable drawer of the refrigerator.

The gnarled roots of celeriac normally point down, buried beneath the earth. Peeled of its rough skin, its flesh is mellow, creamy white, and flavorful.

A mess of boiled crabs is festooned with deep-fried julienned celeriac. The avocado-ginger sauce in our recipe is replaced here by clarified butter.

Matchstick Celeriac with Crabs

* * *

This dish is one of our greatest joys on a cold winter night. Gather your friends, have plenty of paper napkins, a loaf of good sourdough bread, and a chilled white wine ready and you'll have a feast to remember.

2 ½ tablespoons salt

2 pounds celeriac, peeled and quartered

Oil for frying

12 blue crabs

Parsley sprigs for garnish

1 cup avocado-ginger sauce
(see recipe, page 268)

In a large saucepan, bring to a boil 4 quarts of water to which the salt has been added. Meanwhile, julienne the celeriac in a food processor. ❖ *Fill a deep-fryer to ¾ of its capacity with oil and heat to 360 degrees.* ❖ *When the oil is hot, add half the celeriac and cook until golden brown. Drain on paper towels, then place on an ovenproof platter and keep warm in a very low oven while frying the remaining celeriac. Keep the celeriac warm while cooking the crabs.* ❖ *Add the crabs to the boiling water. Once the water boils again, cook the crabs for 8 minutes. Drain.* ❖ *Remove the platter of celeriac from the oven. Gather the celeriac into a mound and surround with the crabs. Garnish with parsley and serve immediately with avocado-ginger sauce.* ❖ *Yield: 4 servings*

KOHLRABI

Several years ago, a man named Barry Beneppe had the brilliant idea to develop outdoor produce markets in New York City. The markets, called Greenmarkets, have been very successful. Not only have they given local farmers an opportunity to sell their freshest produce directly to enthusiastic city dwellers, the markets have also introduced many forgotten vegetables to a city that had been seeing too many plastic-wrapped tomatoes.

Marianne and I frequent all the Greenmarkets on a regular basis; at the Union Square Greenmarket, we came across kohlrabi, a light green or purple vegetable that looks like a bulbous root topped with broad green leaves. Waverley Root, in his book entitled *Food*, tells us that it is one of the oldest vegetables known to man. From ancient Rome to nineteenth-century Britain, kohlrabi has been nourishing kings and paupers. But my own grandmother, an authority on everything that grows in a *potager* (a backyard vegetable garden), taught me that kohlrabi is *not* a root vegetable, but a swelling of the stem just above the ground and a member of the cabbage family. Whatever it is, we have found it delicious, raw or cooked, so thank you, Barry!

AVAILABILITY:
All year round.

SHOPPING GUIDE:
Select small, firm bulbs with no blemishes.

STORAGE:
Will keep for 4 to 5 days, wrapped in plastic, in the vegetable drawer of the refrigerator.

These ridged, bright green kohlrabi, recently rediscovered and prized for their crisp bite, grow above the ground. Their leaves, once cooked, taste similar to kale.

Salad of Kohlrabi and Tamarillo with Pecans

◆ ◆ ◆

The tamarillo is a lovely, egg-shaped fruit with a satiny, thin yellow or red skin and several small seeds. Its flesh is tangy yet sweet, reminiscent of guava. Its flavor blends remarkably well with kohlrabi.

4 kohlrabi bulbs, peeled and julienned

½ pound shelled pecans

3 tamarillos, peeled and sliced*

1 tablespoon lemon juice

2 tablespoons olive oil

Salt and pepper

2 sprigs fresh coriander, leaves only

* Be sure to peel the tamarillos; the skin can be excessively bitter. To peel tamarillos, dip for 1 minute in boiling water, refresh under cold water, and drain. The skin will slip off easily.

Toss together the kohlrabi, pecans, and tamarillos. ❖ *Make a lemon vinaigrette by mixing together the lemon juice, oil, and salt and pepper to taste. Pour over the vegetables and toss well.* ❖ *Just before serving, sprinkle with coriander leaves.* ❖ Yield: 4 servings

....

A little hill of shredded kohlrabi wears an exotic crown of tamarillo. Its slopes are studded with pecans; a lemony vinaigrette accentuates the bittersweet fruitiness of the dish.

Persimmons Stuffed with Kohlrabi Puree

◆ ◆ ◆

2 kohlrabi bulbs, peeled and quartered

4 persimmons

1 tablespoon brandy

2 tablespoons honey, or more if desired

2 sprigs fresh mint, leaves only

Place the kohlrabi in a saucepan and cover with water. Bring to a boil, lower the heat, and simmer about 15 minutes, or until tender. Drain. ❖ *Slice 1 inch off the top of the persimmons. With a spoon, remove the flesh and reserve, being careful not to break the skin.* ❖ *Place the persimmon flesh, kohlrabi, brandy, and honey in the bowl of a food processor. Puree until smooth. Transfer the mixture to a bowl and add more honey if necessary.* ❖ *Fill the persimmon shells with the puree, garnish with mint leaves, and refrigerate until ready to serve.* ❖ Yield: 4 servings

A hollowed persimmon is filled with a puree of honeyed kohlrabi. This alchemist's dessert is garnished with thinly sliced star fruit.

The contrast of textures in this refreshing dessert is the result of a clever mix of fruit and vegetable. Sliced feijoa, sweet cherries, and raw julienned kohlrabi are tossed with honey, brandy, and tangerine juice, and garnished with a lemon wedge, mint, and a pansy.

Salad of Kohlrabi, Feijoa, and Cherries

◆ ◆ ◆

Feijoa is an egg-shaped fruit with a wonderful taste of…"Pineapple," said Marianne…"Concord grapes," replied Greg as he bit into one. Others say it tastes like guava with an aftertaste of lemon. Whatever one may think feijoa tastes like, a salad of kohlrabi with feijoa as a dessert is both unusual and refreshing.

4 kohlrabi bulbs, peeled and julienned

4 feijoas, washed and sliced

1 pound Bing or other sweet red cherries, pitted

1 tablespoon honey

1 tablespoon brandy

1 cup tangerine juice

Edible flowers, such as nasturtium, borage, or pansies, for garnish

Divide the kohlrabi, feijoas, and cherries among 4 individual serving plates. ❖ *In a bowl, mix together the honey, brandy, and tangerine juice. Pour over the fruit salad, garnish with a flower, and serve.* ❖ Yield: 4 servings

JÍCAMA

Lucy Pica joined our family nearly twenty years ago from the small village of Santa Margarita, about twenty miles from Cartagena, Colombia. Although Lucy, a short, rotund woman in her forties, didn't speak a word of English, she quickly managed to take over the running of our household. She'd decide what we were having for dinner and then make me a list of the ingredients she needed. Those I didn't recognize, my daughter Cecile, who was studying Spanish, would translate. Lucy created dinners my friends envied. Her pot roast was famous, her stuffed potatoes delectable, and her *arroz con pollo* a masterpiece of tradition.

Lucy seldom ventured outside our neighborhood until one of her nieces came to visit. Sofia was young and adventurous; very soon, she knew New York like the back of her hand. One day, Sofia announced that she had discovered a Spanish market on 125th Street that had everything: malanga, cassava, jícama, hot peppers, plantains. Lucy's eyes shone with pleasure. "*Sabado*," she announced, "we see."

The following Saturday, the whole family piled into the car for a trip to the Spanish market. Situated under the elevated railroad arches, the market extended for at least six blocks. We passed stalls selling fruits and vegetables I had never seen before: red and green bananas, strange brown roots, cherimoya, and feijoa. Tall sugar canes were being cut with a machete, and women were arguing about prices with merchants in staccato Spanish. Lucy walked through the market like a queen surveying her kingdom. When I questioned her about what looked like an overgrown brown turnip, she said, "Jícama!" and no more. We bought several, but not before she had examined them carefully, scratching the skin with her fingernail.

That night Lucy prepared a dessert of thinly sliced jícama and papaya sprinkled with lime juice. The jícama's sweet taste and crunchy texture reminded me of water chestnuts. Pleased that we all liked jícama, Lucy often prepared it, braising it with artichokes, sautéing it with chicken, and stuffing it with chopped beef. Lucy has left us, now that the kids are grown, but we still prepare jícama the way she taught us to.

It's true: we learned to like jícama because of dear old Lucy. And although the vegetable has become a staple in my mother's kitchen, I must reveal one of Colette's shortcomings here. It's a minor one, so I don't let it bother me too much. It's her pronunciation of the word "jícama." We all know that it is pronounced HEE-*ca-mah. My mother, on the other hand, insists on saying* hee-CA-*mah. And right in front of Lucy! After all these years, when I correct her, she just stares at me for a moment and continues talking, as if there's nothing the matter. One thing keeps me from getting mad: her jícama chips with baby artichokes. That combination leaves me speechless with delight.*

As for the crisp, refreshing vegetable itself, a jícama by any other name would certainly taste as good, especially julienned and tossed with a sweetened cherry coulis.

AVAILABILITY:
All year round.

SHOPPING GUIDE:
Select smooth roots. Scratch the skin: it should be thin, revealing crisp, juicy flesh. Avoid softness, bruises, and dark spots.

STORAGE:
Will keep for 5 to 6 days, wrapped, in the refrigerator.

Jícama Chips with Baby Artichokes

◆ ◆ ◆

12 baby artichokes

1 lemon

2 tablespoons olive oil

2 cloves garlic, peeled and sliced

Salt and pepper

1 teaspoon fresh rosemary leaves

1/2 cup chicken broth

1 large jícama, peeled and thinly sliced (about 1 pound)

Oil for frying

Prepare the artichokes with the lemon as described on page 223. ❖ *In a heavy saucepan, heat the olive oil with the garlic. When the garlic turns a light brown, add the artichokes and sauté for several minutes. Add salt and pepper to taste, the rosemary, and the chicken broth. Bring to a boil, lower the heat, and simmer for 20 minutes.* ❖ *Meanwhile, dry the jícama slices between layers of paper toweling.* ❖ *Fill a deep-fryer to 3/4 of its capacity with oil and heat to 360 degrees. Add some jícama slices and deep-fry until golden brown. Remove with a slotted spoon and keep warm in a very low oven until all the jícama slices are fried.* ❖ *Place the artichoke hearts in the center of a round serving platter. Surround with the jícama chips. Sprinkle with salt and serve.* ❖ *Yield: 4 servings*

Jícama Anna with Mâche

◆ ◆ ◆

Pommes Anna is a delectable French dish made with very thinly sliced potatoes that are layered with butter and baked. The center of the potato cake is soft and fragrant, while the edges are crisp and delicate. One day, as we were preparing dinner, we got a call letting us know there would be a guest for dinner. We looked at one another in dismay. All we had in mind was an improvised meal of vegetables left over from a photography shoot. The only other ingredient on hand was mâche. We thought of serving *pommes Anna* with mâche as a first course, but we had no potatoes. We *did* have lots of jícama, though, so we took the risk. The result brought praise from all!

1 tablespoon vegetable oil

2 large jícamas (about 2 pounds)

Salt and pepper

3 tablespoons butter, at room temperature

½ tablespoon grated lemon rind

1 tablespoon raspberry vinegar

2 tablespoons olive oil

1 clove garlic, peeled and minced

½ pound mâche, rinsed and dried

Preheat the oven to 425 degrees.
❖ *Line a cookie sheet with aluminum foil and brush with the vegetable oil. On the cookie sheet, form 6 circular "flowers" with overlapping jícama slices. Sprinkle with salt and pepper to taste. Cut half of the butter into small pieces and dot each flower with butter.* ❖ *Bake for 8 minutes, or until the edges of the jícama are brown. Turn off the oven, and leave them in oven until ready to serve.* ❖ *Place the remaining butter with the lemon rind in the bowl of a food processor and puree. Transfer to a bowl and refrigerate until* ready to serve. ❖ *Make a vinaigrette by combining the raspberry vinegar, olive oil, garlic, salt and pepper to taste. Toss the mâche with the vinaigrette.* ❖ *Using a spatula, transfer the jícama flowers onto 6 individual serving plates. Dot each flower with lemon butter. Surround with mâche and serve.* ❖ Yield: 6 servings

Thin slices of baked jícama form the delicate petals of a flower, garnished with pitted black olives. The velvety mâche adds a cooling note.

TURNIP

I can still remember my first dinner party in New York. We had just settled into a small apartment on the Upper West Side of Manhattan. I combed the neighborhood in search of a butcher or a greengrocer but found neither. In those days, the only shopping available was at a large neighborhood supermarket. So I examined the cuts of meat wrapped in plastic, trying to figure out what they were. The beef roast looked nothing like a French *rosbif*, I couldn't find an *entrecôte*, and the porterhouse was undeniably expensive (so much for *steak pommes frites!*). I did, however, recognize neatly cut cubes of stewing lamb. I would make *navarin à la printanière*, a French lamb stew with carrots, onions, and turnips.

A *navarin* is cooked slowly until the meat is tender and the vegetables have absorbed the flavors of spices and herbs. When my husband came home from work, he lifted the casserole's lid, sniffed, and uttered, with a cry of disgust, "Lamb stew and turnips! . . . Colette," he intoned with a frown, "you are French and my friends expect a French dinner!" Nothing I could say would change his mind. In his eyes, I had made a monumental faux pas. We didn't talk to each other until the guests arrived and, even then, were coldly polite.

I served dinner, albeit with some trepidation. My *navarin* was a great success! Everyone talked about the delicious turnips...so tasty and tender. When our guests left, my husband apologized. I accepted graciously, and made him do the dishes.

Nowadays, turnips are harvested when very young. American nouvelle cuisine has adopted baby turnips; they have finally taken their rightful place in every chef's repertoire. Their sprightly, nutty flavor comes alive when the root is julienned raw and added to salads, or braised, pureed, or cooked alongside a juicy roast.

AVAILABILITY:
All year round; best in late fall and spring.

SHOPPING GUIDE:
Select small, plump, smooth-skinned turnips with fresh-looking leaves, if possible.

STORAGE:
Will keep for 6 to 7 days, wrapped in plastic, in the vegetable drawer of the refrigerator.

A turnip. This classic root vegetable, which is now harvested very young, is peppery and crisp when eaten raw. Cooked, its flavor mellows.

Glazed pearl onions are nestled in a trio of scooped-out baby turnips. A sprig of laurel adorns the dish.

Turnips Stuffed with Glazed Pearl Onions

❖ ❖ ❖

8 medium-sized turnips

3 tablespoons butter

1/2 cup chicken broth

Salt and pepper

2 tablespoons sugar

18 pearl onions, peeled (1/2 pound)

1 teaspoon chopped fresh chives

Sprigs of parsley for garnish

Peel the turnips. Cut a thin slice off the bottom of each turnip so it can sit on a plate. Using a small spoon, make a large well in the center of each turnip and discard the flesh. ❖ *In a saucepan, melt the butter. When the butter is hot, add the turnips and brown on all sides. Add the chicken broth and salt and pepper to taste. Bring to a boil, lower the heat, and simmer for 10 minutes, or until tender. Using a slotted spoon, transfer to a platter and keep warm, reserving the broth.* ❖ *In a heavy saucepan, dissolve the sugar in 1/4 cup of the turnip cooking liquid. Just before the sugar begins to color, add the onions. Cook for 2 minutes and carefully transfer the onions to a plate.* ❖ *Fill the turnips with the onions, sprinkle with chives, garnish with parsley, and serve.*
❖ *Yield: 4 servings*

JERUSALEM ARTICHOKE, OR SUNCHOKE

It was many years ago, when I was still under my mother's roof and wing, that I first sampled the root of a sunflower. It was a time when—in the realm of food—I was my mother's wide-eyed minion and followed her from market to kitchen, where she assigned chores that I eagerly carried out. She was magician and explorer, and bade me taste an expertly peeled knob of an odd-shaped tuber before tossing the rest into a dish of veau braisé. Boy, did I relish that cold, crisp, sweet, nutty knob! Why she called them sunchokes, I couldn't guess, but it mattered little to me then. When my friends came over after school, I served them sunchokes and Japanese tea instead of the usual Yodels and milk—very bohemian and très risqué—and they were impressed.

Strangely, for a period between the tenth grade and the recent birth of my son, the sunchoke faded from my mind. I did not notice them in the market, nor did they pop up in the many new recipes I tried or tasted. No, I was no longer a bohemian, but a shameless yuppie, scorning the simple knobs of this earth for the more sophisticated miniature vegetables and the sunchoke's lookalike, ginger.

Recently, however, I've taken a step back to hippiedom. I've let my hair grow long, I wear ratty jeans, and I eat sunchokes sautéed with miso and brown rice. My mother doesn't approve of the hair or the jeans, but she is pleased with the recipes I've come up with. By the way, she and lots of other people call them sunchokes because: sunflower root + artichoke taste = sunchoke. They never did come from Jerusalem; rather, the tuber is an American native. It is believed by some that "Jerusalem" comes from girasole, the Italian word for sunflowers. I, for one, suspect that it was an attempt long ago by a savvy promoter to render them exotic.

AVAILABILITY:
All year round.

SHOPPING GUIDE:
Select knobs that are large and crisp. Avoid those with dark or soft spots or mold.

STORAGE:
Will keep for 1 week, wrapped in plastic, in any cool place.

Nubby, bulbous Jerusalem artichokes surprise us with a crisp, translucent, sweet flesh that is equally good raw or cooked.

Giant Endive "Daisy" with Jerusalem Artichokes

◆ ◆ ◆

8 heads Belgian endive

I pound Jerusalem artichokes, peeled

2 cups (5 ounces) alfalfa sprouts

I tablespoon lemon juice

3 tablespoons olive oil

I clove garlic, peeled and minced

Salt and pepper

One 3 ½ -ounce jar black
lumpfish caviar

Separate, rinse, and dry the endive leaves. On a large round platter, create a giant daisy, leaving the center open. ❖ *Using a very small melon baller, shape the Jerusalem artichoke flesh into small round balls. Place the alfalfa sprouts in the center of the daisy. Top with the Jerusalem artichoke balls.* ❖ *In a small bowl, combine the lemon juice, olive oil, garlic, and salt and pepper to taste.* ❖ *Drizzle the sauce over the endives, sprouts, and Jerusalem artichokes. Sprinkle with lumpfish caviar and serve.* ❖ *Yield: 4 to 6 servings*

....

A mound of Jerusalem artichokes, cut with a tiny melon baller to resemble pearls, is strewn with alfalfa sprouts, forming the heart of a daisy created from endives.

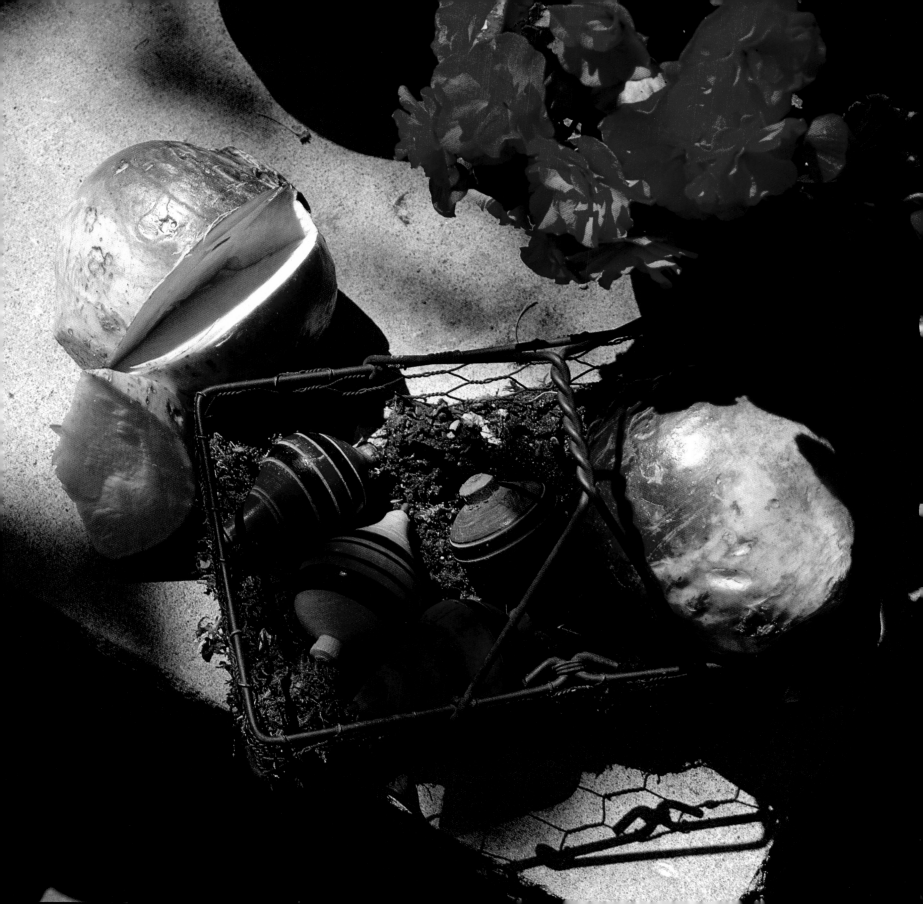

RUTABAGA

A romantic. From the age of twelve until the age of twenty-one, I was to be described as a romantic by my mother, with an understanding and slightly exasperated smile. Of course, I have come to realize that from mother to daughter many things are transferred, and that there is a reason I had such a romantic view of things. After all, when your own mother dries your teenage tears with the assurance that your breasts would one day grow to be as luscious as Jaffa oranges, and smell as sweet, and that your eyes were exactly like those of an Arabian princess, and that a dark and dusky lad would one day take you with him on his worldwide voyages, you end up having a rather dreamy image of the future.

My mother didn't stop at oranges, either. Even vegetables were part of my mother's story of love. She recounted, over and over again, how she won my father's heart with a perfectly prepared tomato salad. And how her rival destroyed her own chances by serving him a dreadful endive gratin for Sunday supper. I grew up believing that knowing how to whip up a soft and fluffy omelet hiding wild mushrooms and dusted with chervil would most assuredly aid me in finding a mate. And that, when I shed tears of melancholy, I should prepare myself a bowl of rutabaga puree. Yes, the peasant in my mother knew that the sweet, earthy, satisfying root would assuage any bitterness in the heart. And she, I maintain, is right. Rutabaga, that homely, heavy, waxed ball, is the stuff of dreams when prepared correctly. Although sometimes called Swedish or Russian turnip, rutabaga has no relation to the turnip but is rather an offshoot of the cabbage family. It requires a delicate hand, yet one strong enough to peel it and cut through its solid flesh. A grating of nutmeg, a spoonful of cream, a pinch of pepper, and the yellow puree is ready to be enjoyed.

Why has rutabaga been relegated to a grandmother's country pantry, to be tossed into a soup along with ham hocks and overgrown onions? Thomas Jefferson was a farmer who loved rutabaga and recognized its culinary merits. Certainly supermarket produce managers, who pile them in a corner below the eye-level cold shelves, are partially to blame for the rutabaga's invisibility. And you might argue, too, that the rutabaga can't compete with "new wave" baby vegetables in elegance or color. But all the romantics of this world have recently united and the rutabaga is coming back into vogue.

My mother and I haven't stopped at puree. The rutabaga can be boiled, baked, and sautéed. It can be cut up and placed around a roast pork while baking or pureed and topped with bits of crisp bacon. Now that I have my lads, I think I'm less romantic than I used to be. But rutabaga still figures in my dreams.

AVAILABILITY:
All year round; best July to April.

SHOPPING GUIDE:
Select smooth-skinned, firm roots that feel heavy for their size.

STORAGE:
Will keep for weeks or even months in a cool, airy place, since commercial rutabagas are dipped in edible wax.

◄ You need a heavy cleaver and even a little muscle power to cut into it, but the rutabaga rewards with a rich, smooth flavor. Here, rutabaga shares a sun-blessed basket with hand-painted Mexican tops in a New York City garden.

Vegetable Pâté with Rutabaga

◆ ◆ ◆

Rutabaga is the perfect binding agent for a vegetable pâté that will hold together without any meat. To serve this pâté as an elegant appetizer, pour some fresh tomato coulis on a salad plate and place a slice on top. This pâté will keep, refrigerated, for several days.

1 rutabaga (about 1 pound), peeled and
cut into 2-inch pieces

Salt and pepper

3 medium carrots, scraped and julienned

4 leeks, trimmed, washed, and sliced

4 small turnips, peeled and
coarsely chopped

1/4 pound green beans, trimmed

4 cups spinach, washed and
coarsely chopped

1 tablespoon dried tarragon

1 tablespoon dried thyme

1/4 cup breadcrumbs

3 eggs

1/4 cup heavy cream

Pinch of nutmeg

2 cups tomato coulis
(see recipe, page 270)

Place the rutabaga in a saucepan, cover with water, add 1/2 teaspoon salt, and bring to a boil uncovered. Reduce the heat to medium and cook, until tender, about 20 minutes. Drain and puree in a food processor. Set aside. ❖ Cook and puree the carrots, leeks, turnips, and green beans in the same manner, blanch the spinach, squeeze, and puree. ❖ Season all the vegetables with salt and pepper to taste. Season the carrot and turnip purees with thyme, and season the green bean puree with tarragon. ❖ Butter a 9 x 5-inch loaf pan and cover the bottom with the breadcrumbs. Beat the eggs with the cream and add to the rutabaga puree. Add salt and pepper to taste and a pinch of nutmeg. Mix well. ❖ Preheat the oven to 400 degrees. ❖ Cover the breadcrumbs with about a third of the spinach, then smooth the rutabaga puree over the spinach. Now, smooth the carrot puree over the rutabaga. Continue alternating a vegetable layer with a layer of rutabaga. The last layer should be spinach. Cover the loaf pan with a double layer of aluminum foil and cut a small slit in the center for the steam to escape. ❖ Place the loaf pan in a roasting pan. Add enough hot water to go 2 inches up the side of the loaf pan. Bake for 1/2 hour. Take the pan out of the oven. Arrange several heavy cans on top to weigh the pâté down. Cool at room temperature for several hours, then refrigerate overnight. ❖ Unmold the pâté onto a small platter and slice. Serve with tomato coulis. ❖ Yield: 10 servings

This pâté, a mosaic of vegetables bound by pureed rutabaga, makes an unusual summertime appetizer. The brilliant color of the coulis comes from peak-season fresh tomatoes. ▶

Rutabaga Stuffed with Black Beans

◆ ◆ ◆

Serve this dish on a cold Sunday for brunch with toasted bagels and a salad of Belgian endive or beets. You can find fresh eels in Chinese fish stores or canned eels from Spain in gourmet shops.

4 rutabagas (³⁄₄ pound each)

Salt and pepper

2 tablespoons butter

1 tablespoon light soy sauce

1 16-ounce can black beans

1 ¹⁄₂ tablespoons olive oil*

Juice of 1 lemon

¹⁄₄ teaspoon ground cumin

¹⁄₄ teaspoon hot red-pepper flakes

2 ounces fresh or canned baby eels (optional)

Parsley sprigs for garnish

*If you are using canned eels, use the oil in the can to heat the beans instead of the olive oil.

Peel the rutabagas. Using a melon baller, scoop out enough flesh to form a large cavity in the center of each one. Cut a thin slice off the bottom of each rutabaga so that it can sit on a plate. ❖ Bring 2 quarts of water to a boil; add ¹⁄₂ teaspoon salt and cook the rutabagas about 20 to 30 minutes or until tender. Drain. ❖ In a saucepan, melt the butter, add the rutabagas, and sauté for 3 to 4 minutes. Add the soy sauce and sauté for another minute. Season with salt and pepper to taste. Set aside. ❖ Drain and rinse the black beans. Heat with the olive oil and add lemon juice to taste. Season with salt, cumin, and pepper flakes, then add the eels and simmer for 3 minutes. ❖ Place the rutabagas on a serving platter. Fill the cavities with the black-bean mixture and garnish with parsley. ❖ Yield: 4 servings

....

A hollowed-out rutabaga is an edible dish filled with highly seasoned black beans and tiny eels imported from Spain. We have a penchant for unlaid chicken eggs, one of which garnishes this rich vegetable creation. A hard-boiled quail egg would make an equally amusing garnish.

Rutabaga and Leek Puree

• • •

This flavorful puree can be served for brunch with poached eggs or for dinner with broiled lamb chops.

1 rutabaga, peeled and quartered (1 ½ pounds)

Salt and pepper

4 leeks, washed and trimmed

2 tablespoons butter

½ cup heavy cream

½ tablespoon chopped fresh parsley

½ cup sugar

1 carambola (star fruit), sliced, for garnish

Place the rutabaga in a large saucepan and cover with water. Add ½ teaspoon salt and bring to a boil. Reduce the heat to medium and cook for 30 minutes, or until the rutabaga can be pierced with a fork. Drain. ❖ *Slice 3 of the leeks across at 2-inch intervals. Slice only the white part of the fourth leek. Reserve the green part.* ❖ *Place the leeks in a saucepan, cover with water, bring to a boil, reduce the heat to medium, and cook 15 minutes, or until tender. Drain, reserving the liquid for another use.* ❖ *Place the rutabaga with the leeks, butter, and cream in the bowl of a food processor and puree. Transfer the puree to a saucepan and correct the seasoning. Add the parsley.* ❖ *Cut the green part of the fourth leek lengthwise into very thin strips. Place the sugar and 3 tablespoons of water in a small saucepan. Slowly melt the sugar over medium heat, stirring constantly. When the sugar begins to take on a gold color, add the leek strips and glaze for 1 minute. Arrange on aluminum foil with a slotted spoon.* ❖ *Just before serving, heat the puree. Transfer to a large serving bowl. Garnish with the glazed leeks and the sliced carambola.* ❖ *Yield: 4 servings*

Served in a Mexican earthenware dish, this rutabaga and leek puree is enhanced by lemony sliced star fruit. Ribbons of fried leek are crunchy and slightly sweet. Broiled lamb chops accompany this light and smooth puree.

PARSLEY ROOT

The first time I bought parsley root, I mistook it for a bunch of parsnips with the leaves still attached. I was astonished to discover that the leaves tasted just like parsley! Thumbing through my books, I realized that what I had on my kitchen counter wasn't parsnips but parsley root, a.k.a. Hamburg parsley (it is very popular in Central Europe). I reassured myself that even for a self-proclaimed vegetable expert, the error was natural. The main differences between the two are that parsley root is narrower than parsnip, and its flesh is grayish white rather than creamy yellow. Well, I tried parsley root braised, baked, and sautéed with mushrooms. Each dish was successful, but Marianne's response said it all: "So what! I prefer parsnips." Challenged, I presented her with a platter of thinly sliced, deep-fried parsley root garnished with fried parsley and sprinkled with coarse salt. She gobbled it up and praised me for five straight minutes—a rare occurrence, I must say.

Parsley root is excellent julienned in a rich chicken broth or used in any recipe calling for either parsnips or carrots. When preparing parsley root, have a bowl of acidulated water on hand. Like artichoke and burdock, parsley root turns brown on contact with the air. Use parsley root leaves as you would regular parsley; their more pronounced flavor make them an ideal addition to soups and sauces.

AVAILABILITY:
All year round.

SHOPPING GUIDE:
Select roots that are plump and firm with fresh deep-green leaves.

STORAGE:
The leaves will keep for 3 to 4 days, lightly moistened and wrapped in paper towels in the vegetable drawer of the refrigerator; the root will keep for up to 1 week, wrapped and refrigerated.

Parsley root can be confused with the parsnip, which it resembles uncannily. The difference is that parsley root has real parsley—sweet and sprightly—as its top.

Parsley Root Chips

• • •

Serve these with drinks before dinner or as a side dish with broiled steak.

3 parsley roots

Juice of 1 lemon

Oil for frying

Parsley sprigs from parsley root

Salt and pepper

Cut off the leaves of the parsley roots, wash, and pat dry. Set aside to dry thoroughly. ❖ *Peel the roots and thinly slice. Drop the slices in a bowl of cold water mixed with the lemon juice.* ❖ *Fill a deep, heavy skillet or deep-fryer to its capacity and heat oil to 350 degrees. Drain the parsley root and pat dry with paper towels.* ❖ *Fry the slices, about a dozen at a time, until golden brown, about 30 seconds. Drain on paper towels and keep warm in a very low oven.* ❖ *When all the slices have been fried, drop sprigs of parsley leaves in the hot oil and fry until just before they turn brown, a few seconds. Drain on paper towels.* ❖ *Place the root slices in a bowl, add salt and pepper to taste, and toss well. Serve piping hot garnished with fried parsley.* ❖ *Yield: 4 servings*

The best part about parsley root is that both leaves and root are used in cooking. Here, they are deep fried.

PARSNIP

The parsnip is a long, beige-colored root, shaped like a large carrot. Until the potato became a staple in Europe in the nineteenth century, the parsnip was eaten in abundance, especially during Lent, as they are more nourishing than carrots or turnips. Alas, the world more or less forgot the parsnip for more than 100 years, except for French peasants, who tossed a few into their pot-au-feu, and British traditionalists, who favored the root mashed with butter and double cream. Rediscovered by the innovators of nouvelle cuisine, the parsnip is back on menus and enjoys a tentative popularity.

The parsnip is excellent braised with Belgian endive, pureed with blue cheese, in soups, and in tempura. When cooked, parsnips are sweet and richly flavored, unless you eat them before the first frost, when they are bitter.

AVAILABILITY:
All year round; best October to April.

SHOPPING GUIDE:
Select small or medium parsnips that are plump and crisp. Avoid those with cracks, discolorations, shriveled skin, or softness.

STORAGE:
Will keep for 4 to 5 days, wrapped in plastic, in the vegetable drawer of the refrigerator.

Parsnips, long forgotten, have garnered new favor in recent years. Our robot mascot is holding a sheaf of lemon grass that will perfume a parsnip puree.

A twist on traditional guacamole: a puree of
parsnips is seasoned with lime juice
and coriander.

Parsnip Puree with Avocado

◆ ◆ ◆

2 pounds parsnips, peeled
and quartered

Salt and pepper

1 ½ cups Italian flat-leaf parsley leaves,
washed

2 cloves garlic, peeled

4 tablespoons butter

½ avocado, seeded and peeled

One 3 ½-ounce package enoki
mushrooms, trimmed

*Place the parsnips in a saucepan, cover with wa-
ter, and add 1 teaspoon salt. Bring to a boil, lower
the heat to medium, and cook for 15 minutes, or
until tender. Drain.* ❖ *Place the parsnips,
parsley, and garlic in the bowl of a food processor
and puree. Pour back into the saucepan. Add the
butter and salt and pepper to taste. Keep warm
until ready to serve.* ❖ *Pour the puree into a
serving bowl. Very thinly slice the avocado. Make
a flower with the slices by arranging them around
the bowl like petals. Cut ½ inch from the enoki
stems and place them either on the edges of the
bowl or in the center of the flower.*
❖ *Yield: 4 servings*

Braised Parsnips with Baby Artichokes and Red Pepper Sauce

◆ ◆ ◆

¹/₄ pound dried shiitake mushrooms

1 pound baby artichokes

Juice of ¹/₂ lemon

3 tablespoons olive oil

1 tablespoon butter

1 clove garlic, peeled and sliced

2 pounds parsnips, peeled and
cut into 2-inch pieces

2 tablespoons sugar

1 teaspoon dried sage

Salt and pepper

1 ¹/₂ cups red pepper sauce
(see recipe, page 270)

Soak the dried mushrooms in a bowl of lukewarm water for about 20 minutes. Drain, reserving the liquid. Cut off the stems and discard. Set the mushroom caps aside. ❖ *Cut ¹/₂ inch from the top of each artichoke. Trim the stems. Cut each artichoke in half lengthwise. Place in a bowl of cold water with the lemon juice.* ❖ *In a large saucepan, heat the olive oil with the butter. Add the garlic and sauté until light brown. Drain the artichokes and add to the oil. Sauté for 3 minutes, then add the parsnips. Sprinkle the vegetables with the sugar, mix, and cook for 2 minutes. Add half the mushroom water (save the rest for another purpose), the mushroom caps, and the sage. Lower the heat and simmer for 15 minutes, or until the vegetables are tender. Season with salt and pepper to taste. Arrange the parsnips on a platter surrounding the artichokes.* ❖ *Serve with red pepper sauce on the side.* ❖ *Yield: 4 servings*

A vegetable "star" is created with small braised parsnips, shiitake mushrooms, and a baby artichoke. Garlic, sage, and olive oil are among the key seasonings in this dramatic side dish.

CHINESE VEGETABLES

Marianne, her sisters, and her brother went to school in Brooklyn Heights, across the river from Manhattan. By the time Marianne reached the eighth grade, I had become chairperson of the language department of the same school. Every morning, the five of us would trot to the subway together and every afternoon we'd come back together. I don't know how they felt to have their mother along every day, but as soon as the weather got warm, they seemed happier. I think it's because we would walk across the Brooklyn Bridge into Chinatown, stop in a coffee shop, and have dumplings for tea. After tea, we'd stroll down Mott Street, the best shopping street in Chinatown, and together we'd select vegetables for dinner. At first, I wasn't sure what I was buying. Once, Marianne urged me to buy Chinese geranium leaves. I shocked a Chinese friend of ours by popping them into a vase with a few flowers. They were supposed to be boiled in a soup or braised!

As the years went by, I learned more about how to identify and prepare Chinese vegetables. However, I never cooked Chinese style and Marianne was often critical of my attempts to use these unusual vegetables in my own way. She'd say, "It's so much better in Chinatown. . . ."

I kept at it and, today, Marianne seems to approve (and even applaud) my efforts. Happily, a trek to Chinatown isn't always necessary for us since Korean markets in New York City carry many Oriental vegetables. And vegetables such as snow peas, bok choy, bean sprouts, taro, ginger, and fresh coriander are available in many supermarkets.

◄ A purveyor in New York's Chinatown, having risen before dawn to fetch his produce from a Chinese farm in nearby New Jersey, hawks his abundant selection of Chinese vegetables.

Fuzzy melon

Chinese water spinach

Arrowhead

Lotus root

Chinese eggplant

Snow pea

Chinese spinach

Wild rice shoot

Water chestnut

Winter melon

Bitter melon

Chinese long bean

Daikon

Taro

Chinese Cabbage

China has given us such a rich array of vegetables that I will always have a new variety to taste and experiment with. And yet, I have my loyalties. Fuzzy melon, Chinese water spinach, arrowhead, lotus root, Chinese eggplant, and snow peas are my Oriental staples, those that I enjoy playing with and have grown to accept as part of my everyday cuisine. In fact, my dinner guests—all of them—know me as the friend who introduced them to steamed Chinese purple eggplant with ginger sauce, one of my signature dishes. They *expect* the spring green of snow peas to grace their plates, or to munch on raw slices of lotus root dipped in pureed avocado. For those who've always turned their noses up at the metallic taste of spinach, my silky water spinach, sautéed in garlicky olive oil, has changed their outlook altogether. "Colette has traded in her wooden spoon for a pair of giant chopsticks," they say.

From bottom to top: baskets filled with fuzzy ▶
melon, purple Chinese eggplant, and bitter melon.

FUZZY MELON

Walking through Chinatown in the summer, I'm always giving in to the temptation to buy a vegetable I know nothing about. Once, what I thought was a sweet squash turned out to be a medicinal gourd, used to make a fortifying broth for invalids. Fuzzy melon, however, was better than I ever dreamed. Similar to a cucumber in taste, but sweeter, the fuzzy melon is dumbbell-shaped and covered with white fuzz, like a newborn baby's hair. Like summer squash, or young zucchini, it can be eaten raw in salad or sliced for stewing. Julienned and stir-fried, it is delicious served with broiled or barbecued meats.

AVAILABILITY:
March to August.

SHOPPING GUIDE:
Select very young, firm melons, as dark green as possible.

STORAGE:
Will keep for 3 to 4 days in the vegetable drawer of the refrigerator.

An odd-shaped fuzzy melon echoes the shape, if not the texture or taste, of the smaller purple eggplant. The beauty of Chinese vegetables such as these is that they can be combined in myriad ways, each a burst of intriguing contrasts.

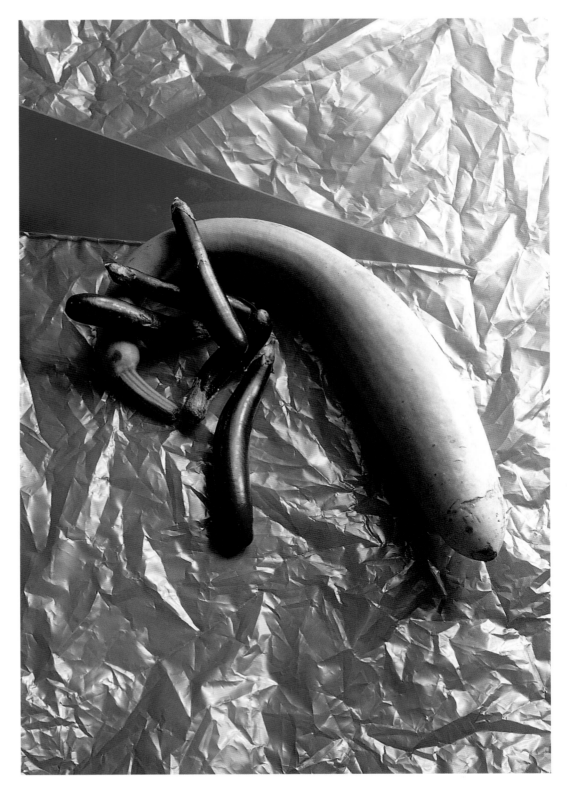

CHINESE WATER SPINACH

I know that spring is not far away when I spot water spinach in Chinatown's produce shops. This spinach, as its name tells us, grows in water. Each long hollow stem has several arrowhead-shaped green leaves that are tender and sweet. In early spring, it can be eaten raw in salad. Because of its high water content, the best way to cook this vegetable is to steam or lightly sauté it for a scant minute, then add olive oil or butter and season with freshly ground pepper or a piquant mustard.

AVAILABILITY:
March to April.

SHOPPING GUIDE:
Select water spinach with relatively short stems and crisp, light green leaves. Allow for shrinkage: water spinach cooks down to a third of its original volume.

STORAGE:
Will keep for no more than 1 to 2 days, wrapped in a plastic bag, in the vegetable drawer of the refrigerator.

Chinese water spinach differs from regular spinach in that it is grown directly in water. Very mild and sweet, its flavor is enhanced by a few drops of lemon juice or a drizzle of fruity olive oil.

ARROWHEAD

This vegetable is a round tuber with what looks like a tail. It is pale brown with a very thin skin. When peeled, its flesh is white. This tuber tastes like a potato; it can be eaten sautéed, braised, steamed, in soup, and added to stews. The arrowhead looks like a tail, and measures one and one-half inches long. It has a very thin skin, similar to the Jerusalem artichoke.

AVAILABILITY:
All year round.

SHOPPING GUIDE:
Select firm, round tubers with no growth on the tail.

STORAGE:
Will keep for 3 to 4 days, wrapped in plastic, in the vegetable drawer of the refrigerator.

A case of mistaken identity! When we photographed these little bulbs with a diving mask and fins, we thought we were dealing with water chestnuts. In actuality, these are *tsee goo*, a.k.a. arrowhead tubers, which resemble the popular water chestnut. So much for vegetable wordplay!

One of the "flowers" of the Chinese vegetable kingdom, lotus root's lacy slices add sweetness and crunch to soups. Its flavor, reminiscent of sunchokes and jícama, stands up to braising and stir-frying as well.

LOTUS ROOT

This vegetable looks like a string of fat sausages. It's a pale pink-brown color, very light because it is hollow. When peeled and cut, lotus root looks lacy, like a flower. It retains its crunchy texture even when cooked. Lotus root can be steamed, sautéed, braised, stir-fried, added to soups, and even eaten raw.

AVAILABILITY:
All year round.

SHOPPING GUIDE:
Select firm, plump roots.

STORAGE:
Will keep for 2 weeks, unwrapped, in the vegetable drawer of the refrigerator.

CHINESE EGGPLANT

I was first attracted to Chinese eggplant because of its color: an almost incandescent, pearly purple that reminded me of my grandmother's much-envied purple velvet dress with tiny white buttons at the collar. At the age of six, I had cut a big piece out of it to make a dress for my doll and I couldn't imagine why she was so angry with me. I kept the piece of purple cloth for years until it faded away and lost its shiny hue. That's what happened to my purple eggplants once I steamed them; they turned a drab brown! I tried other ways of cooking them, to no avail; whether I sautéed, baked, or fried them, they always lost their lovely purple color. Although I've learned to accept this transformation, it still irks me. Happily, their subtle, nutty flavor and lack of seeds make them an ideal vegetable to serve hot or cold with meats and fish or to puree in a soup.

Chinese eggplant is about six to twelve inches long and one and one-half to two inches in diameter. It varies in color from pale to bright purple.

AVAILABILITY:
All year round.

SHOPPING GUIDE:
Select firm, glossy eggplants; narrower ones have fewer seeds.

STORAGE:
Will keep for 3 to 4 days, in a sealed plastic bag, in the vegetable drawer of the refrigerator.

Steamed Chinese Eggplant with Ginger-Scallion Sauce

◆ ◆ ◆

This dish is excellent with stuffed chicken breasts (see recipe, page 45). You can also split the eggplant lengthwise and tuck two or three poached oysters in the cleft.

2-inch piece fresh ginger

4 scallions

½ cup oil

Salt and pepper

4 Chinese eggplants

Peel the ginger and cut into small pieces. ❖ Wash, trim, and thinly slice the scallions. Place the scallions, ginger, and oil in the bowl of a food processor and puree. Pour the sauce into a bowl and season with salt and pepper to taste. (This sauce can keep for several days, refrigerated.) ❖ Steam the eggplant for 8 to 10 minutes. ❖ Place 1 eggplant on each of 4 individual serving plates, nap with the ginger-scallion sauce, and serve.
❖ Yield: 4 servings

▲
Chinese eggplants, lightly steamed and served with a frothy ginger-scallion sauce, are the ideal accompaniment to a stuffed chicken breast. Small chilies can be chopped and used sparingly on the tender, mild eggplant.

Chinese Eggplant Soup with Daikon

* * *

This recipe can be made with any eggplant, but it is preferable to make it with the Chinese variety since it has very few seeds and is not bitter. If you use regular eggplant, bake it whole at 325 degrees for twenty minutes, peel it, and proceed as in the recipe. Strain the soup through a fine sieve before serving.

1 ½ pounds Chinese eggplant

2 quarts chicken broth

1 daikon, peeled and quartered

2 cloves garlic, peeled

Salt and pepper

Cumin

Parsley sprigs for garnish

8 slices French baguette, toasted

Cut the stems off the eggplants but do not peel. Slice the eggplants into 3-inch rounds. Bring the chicken broth to a boil and add the eggplant and the daikon. Cook over medium heat for 10 minutes. Transfer to the bowl of a food processor, add the garlic, and puree. Return the soup to the saucepan and season with salt and pepper to taste and a pinch of cumin. ❖ *Pour into individual soup bowls, garnish with parsley, and serve with toasted baguette slices.* ❖ *Yield: 4 servings*

This smooth, hearty soup is simply a marriage of homemade chicken broth and pureed Chinese eggplant, seasoned with garlic and cumin. The bowl in the foreground is garnished with edible flower petals; sprigs of thyme top the other.

SNOW PEA

For a long time, I shied away from snow peas. As an "expert" on Chinese vegetables, I considered snow peas to occupy the lowest rung of the Chinese vegetable ladder, as common and ordinary as chow mein. My current love for the flat, tender pea is due to a Spanish artist who goes by the name Miralda. He asked me to join him in a food "happening," an event that he dubbed "A Thanksgiving Dinner for the Bronx Zoo." Each participant was to create a dish for a particular animal in the zoo, using ingredients taken directly from their true, in-the-wild diet. I was assigned the flamingos and was told that they thrive on carotene. So I filled a pumpkin with carrot soup—lots of carotene there—but had to find a way to make it appealing to the flamingos. Miralda suggested snow peas, since I could trim them into any shape I wished. I lined a plate with Chinese chives to create "grass," placed the pumpkin on top, and arranged snow peas, cut to look like small fish, among the chive "grass." The flamingos ate the soup and I was left with a whole bag of snow peas. That evening, I sautéed them with fresh basil and pine nuts and everyone loved them. I loved them. And I still love them. I stuff them with fish, add them to consommé, and serve them raw with yogurt dip.

Snow peas are available everywhere, in supermarkets as well as Oriental and other produce markets.

AVAILABILITY:
All year round.

SHOPPING GUIDE:
Select small, firm, shiny pods with minuscule peas. Avoid shriveled or limp pods.

STORAGE:
Will keep for 2 days, loosely packed in a plastic bag, in the vegetable drawer of the refrigerator.

Stuffed Snow Peas

◆ ◆ ◆

1 pound firm-fleshed fish, such as bass, pike, or sole, cooked and mashed

1 egg

½ tablespoon chopped fresh parsley

½ teaspoon sesame oil

Salt and pepper

1 pound snow peas

5 leaves Boston lettuce or cabbage

½ pound dried wood ear mushrooms soaked in warm water for 30 minutes

1 cup chicken broth

½ tablespoon olive oil

6 to 8 Chinese garlic chive flowers

1 cup parsley sauce (see recipe, page 270)

In a bowl, combine the fish, egg, parsley, sesame oil, salt and a generous amount of pepper. ❖ *Trim the snow peas. Using scissors, cut a thin strip along one side to open the snow pea. Using a demitasse spoon, stuff each pea with fish paste.* ❖ *Line a steamer with lettuce or cabbage leaves. Place the snow peas on top, side by side, and steam for 5 minutes. Set aside.* ❖ *Drain the mushrooms. Boil them for 5 minutes in the chicken broth. Drain. Toss the mushrooms with the oil, salt, and pepper.* ❖ *Line a serving platter with the mushrooms. Arrange the stuffed snow peas on top. Garnish with the flowering chives and serve with parsley sauce.* ❖ *Yield: 4 to 6 servings*

....

Snow peas, sweet and tender, become "boats" carrying a cargo of seasoned fish. A "sea" is created with wood ear mushrooms tossed with olive oil. Garlic chive flowers season the dish and make an unusual flower arrangement as well. ▶

CHINESE SPINACH, OR EEN CHOY

For many years, I hated spinach! Looking back, I'm not surprised: it was chopped, stewed, cooked to death, and nothing could induce me to swallow bitter green mush. When my children were growing up, I never prepared spinach at home, to my mother-in-law's consternation. To my deaf ears, she would claim that spinach was good for my children's blood. I didn't even relent when Marianne's teacher called to complain that Marianne never ate her spinach, and was a bad example to the other students. I defended Marianne, saying that she was absolutely right to not eat the hateful stuff! But a few years ago, we were guests of my friend Edith, whose vegetable garden I have always envied. That fateful night, she served a special Chinese spinach with a beautiful red tint, steamed ever so lightly and sprinkled with black sesame seeds. I now love spinach and, if I could, would publicly apologize to Marianne's third-grade teacher!

Chinese spinach is available in Chinese markets and some specialty produce markets. The red variety is milder tasting than the green. Chinese spinach can be steamed, sautéed, stir-fried with garlic, or dropped into hot broth. Chinese spinach grows in bunches that share a common, long pink root. Its broad oval leaves cluster limply at the top of a long stem. These leaves often have a red center that seems almost to be painted on. This red pattern does not fade when the spinach is lightly steamed, so I like to use een choy when I am creating a delicate, painterly dish. Even its flavor is more refined than that of regular spinach.

AVAILABILITY:
April to September.

SHOPPING GUIDE:
Select bunches that look fresh with firm roots. Avoid those with bruised leaves.

STORAGE:
Will keep for 2 days, in a sealed plastic bag, in the vegetable drawer of the refrigerator. If it is to be steamed, best the day it is bought.

◄ There are two varieties of Chinese spinach: red and green. Pictured is the beautiful red-tinted variety, with a smooth—not bitter—flavor and an elegant shape.

Chinese Spinach with Broad Noodles

◆ ◆ ◆

The Chinese make a very wide, white rice noodle, which they roll around tiny shrimp and minced scallions. These filled noodles are sold in the street from steam tables in New York's Chinatown. The noodles themselves are also available in any Chinese grocery store. You can replace them with wide fresh pasta. Toss the shrimp and the scallions with the cooked pasta.

Version One

2 bunches red-leaf Chinese spinach, washed and trimmed

1 tablespoon olive oil

1/2 teaspoon sesame oil

Salt and pepper

8 cooked and filled rice noodles

Bring 2 quarts of salted water to a boil. Add the Chinese spinach, bring back to a boil, and turn off the heat. Let stand for 2 minutes, then drain. Place the spinach in a bowl, add the olive and sesame oils, season with salt and pepper to taste, and toss gently. ❖ Arrange some spinach on each of 4 individual serving plates and garnish with the Chinese rice noodles.

Version Two

2 bunches red-leaf Chinese spinach, washed and trimmed

2 tablespoons olive oil

1 pound wide fresh pasta

1/2 pound cooked small shrimp, cut into tiny pieces

3 scallions, minced

1/2 teaspoon sesame oil

Salt and pepper

Chinese spinach is the dramatic background for rolled rice noodles filled with tiny shrimp. Sesame oil adds a pungent note and a glossy finish.

Cook the Chinese spinach as above. Let stand for 2 minutes, drain, then place in a bowl and set aside. ❖ Bring 2 quarts of salted water with 1/2 teaspoon of olive oil to a boil. Add the pasta and cook for 2 minutes. Drain. ❖ Place the pasta in a bowl and add the shrimp, scallions, and the sesame and remaining olive oils. Season with salt and pepper to taste and toss.
❖ Yield: 4 servings

Chinese Spinach with Ham

• • •

½ cup sugar

3 tablespoons white rum

½ pound fresh kumquats

1 bunch red-leaf Chinese spinach, washed and trimmed (about 1 pound)

1 tablespoon olive oil

Salt

6 slices prosciutto cotto*

6 edible flowers (optional)

*Prosciutto cotto is baked prosciutto and is available in most gourmet delicatessens. You can also substitute smoked ham.

In a large saucepan, bring 2 cups of water to a boil. Add the sugar and cook for 5 minutes, then add the rum and the kumquats. Bring back to a boil, lower the heat, and simmer for 5 minutes. Remove from the heat to cool. Drain. ❖ *Steam the spinach for 1 minute.* ❖ *On each of 6 individual serving plates, arrange a mound of spinach. Brush with olive oil and sprinkle with salt. Garnish with the kumquats. Roll the ham slices decoratively and place next to the spinach. Garnish with an edible flower (if desired).* ❖ *Yield: 6 servings*

The kumquats nesting atop steamed Chinese spinach have been boiled with a bit of sugar yet remain quite tart, perfect with the mild greens and salty prosciutto cotto, rolled and garnished with an edible flower.

WILD RICE SHOOT

Marianne is my most difficult critic, and it takes a great deal of effort on my part to convince her to try a vegetable that she does not know or thinks is too weird.

Intrigued by the spear-like shape of a vegetable I spotted in Chinatown one day, I asked the vendor what it was and his answer was "Chinese asparagus." When I cut into it, I was delighted by the pattern of tiny black dots on white flesh. Raw, it was inedible. So I peeled off the leaves, sliced it, and steamed it. Drizzled with olive oil, it had a pleasing potato flavor with an aftertaste of eggplant. Although I had to coax her first to try it, Marianne raved. But her doubting nature didn't accept my claim that this tender stalk was asparagus. She did some research and explained to me, with extreme satisfaction and in a serious tone, that it was the shoot of wild rice. Then, to my surprise, she congratulated me on my find. I'll never understand my daughter!

AVAILABILITY:
June to September.

SHOPPING GUIDE:
Select firm young shoots with a thick base.

STORAGE:
Will keep for 2 days, in a sealed plastic bag, in the vegetable drawer of the refrigerator. Best eaten the day it is bought.

Young wild rice shoots. The spongy inner core has a light, potatolike taste and absorbs the flavors of whatever seasoning is used to prepare it. Adorning the shoots is a bunch of wild, inedible berries.

Wild Rice Shoots with Pink Garlic

❖ ❖ ❖

12 wild rice shoots

3 tablespoons oil

½ cup pink garlic*

Salt and pepper

*Sweet-tasting pickled garlic is available in Japanese grocery stores. The garlic is blanched, then pickled in vinegar and beet juice.

Sautéed wild rice shoots are combined with pickled pink garlic and julienned spinach to create a complex marriage of flavors in a simple dish.

Remove the outer leaves of the rice shoots and slice crosswise into ½ -inch pieces. In a skillet, heat the oil. When the oil is hot, add the rice shoots and sauté until golden brown on both sides. ❖ *Using a slotted spoon, transfer to a platter. Add the pink garlic and salt and pepper to taste.*

❖ Yield: 4 servings

WATER CHESTNUT

I am an avid gardener. Any time I see a bulb, I grab it, plant it, and hope that some exotic, flaming red, sumptuous flower will emerge to brighten my very shady garden. When I first spied fresh water chestnuts, I bought half a dozen and planted them in the only sunny patch of earth I own. I waited. And waited. Eventually, little, green, unimpressive nubbins showed through the ground. That was all, and I realized that I had forfeited my best garden space to dud bulbs. Later in the summer, I was walking through Chinatown and noticed the same small, brown bulbs taunting me from their crate. The sign above them read WATER CHESTNUTS $3 A POUND. No wonder they hadn't yielded the flowers of my dreams!

Water chestnuts are small, hard, bulb-like roots that end in a point. The outer skin is papery, much like onion skin, and the inner skin is thin, brown, and easy to peel. Its flesh is white and crisp, similar in texture to a radish or jícama. Raw, it is bland in flavor, yet it adds a crisp note to salads and vegetable mixtures. Cooked, the water chestnut is starchy in taste, a perfect addition to stews and braised foods. Canned water chestnuts are an excellent substitute.

It is important to buy more water chestnuts than you think you need; after peeling, they end up quite small, about the size of a walnut. Drop them in acidulated water as soon as you peel them to prevent darkening.

AVAILABILITY:
All year round.

SHOPPING GUIDE:
Select firm, hard water chestnuts. Avoid any that are soft or bruised.

STORAGE:
Will keep for 1 week, peeled and covered in water, in the refrigerator.

These rootlike bulbs (corms, to the botanist) are not cultivated in water as their name suggests. Beneath their brown, papery skin hides a crisp, juicy flesh that turns starchy once cooked.

Here, water chestnuts are gently braised and peppered with green chilies. Prickly pears add a note of color and cool the fire, too.

Braised Fresh Water Chestnuts with Serrano Chilies

• • •

2 pounds fresh water chestnuts

Juice of ½ lemon

2 tablespoons olive oil

1 tablespoon soy sauce

1 cup chicken broth

Salt

3 serrano chilies, seeded and sliced lengthwise

2 prickly pears, peeled and sliced

Peel the water chestnuts and place in a bowl of cold water with the lemon juice. ❖ *In a saucepan, heat the oil. Drain the water chestnuts. When the oil is hot, add the water chestnuts and sauté for 3 to 4 minutes. Add the soy sauce and chicken broth. Bring to a boil, lower the heat, and simmer for 15 minutes. Correct the seasoning.* ❖ *Arrange the water chestnuts on a serving platter. Sprinkle with the sliced chilies, garnish with the prickly pears, and serve.* ❖ *Yield: 4 servings*

WINTER MELON

Winter melon resembles a round watermelon. The outside skin is a deep green and the inside is like a honeydew—a pale white-green. Winter melon is sold by the slice; a two-pound slice will be enough for four servings. Winter melon tastes bland; therefore, it is good in soups, in stews, and fun and unusual when prepared and served as French fries.

AVAILABILITY:
All year round.

SHOPPING GUIDE:
Select winter melon that has not been open for long. The flesh should look fresh and firm.

STORAGE:
Best eaten the day it is bought.

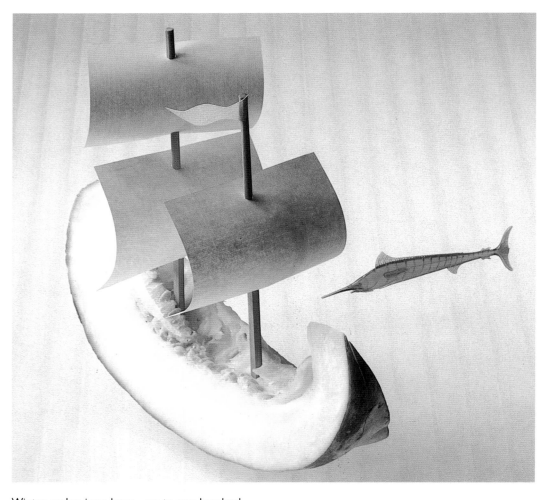

Winter melon is so large—up to one hundred pounds in some cases—that it is often sold cut into wedges. Although it resembles honeydew, winter melon is a bland gourd, far from sweet.

Consommé with Winter Melon

• • •

2 pounds winter melon

2 quarts vegetable broth

12 shrimp balls (see recipe ▼)

4 large shrimp, shelled and deveined

Salt and pepper

1 tablespoon grated lemon or lime zest

Peel the winter melon and cut into thin slices. Cut each slice across into 1-inch pieces. ❖ *In a large saucepan, bring the vegetable broth to a boil, then add the winter melon and the shrimp balls. Bring back to a boil, lower the heat to medium, and cook for 4 minutes. Add the shrimp and cook for another 5 minutes. Adjust seasoning with salt and pepper.* ❖ *Divide the soup among 4 individual soup bowls, add 1 shrimp to each bowl, and garnish with a sprinkling of grated zest.* ❖ Yield: 4 servings

Shrimp Balls

• • •

These delicacies can be bought frozen in most Oriental food markets.

1 pound white-fish fillet, cut into 1-inch pieces

1 pound medium shrimp, shelled and deveined

1 egg

Salt and pepper

2 tablespoons cornstarch

Place the fish, shrimp, egg, and salt and pepper to taste in the bowl of a food processor and puree. Transfer to a bowl, add 1 tablespoon cornstarch, and mix well. If the puree is too loose, add 1 more tablespoon cornstarch. Refrigerate for 2 hours. ❖ *Bring 1 quart of salted water to a boil and lower the heat to simmer. Shape the fish mixture into balls the size of a large grape and drop them into the simmering water. Cook for 5 minutes and drain. Cool and refrigerate until ready to use.* ❖ *These fish-shrimp balls can be frozen.* ❖ Yield: 2 dozen balls

In this light, soothing appetizer, cubes of winter melon and homemade shrimp balls float in a hot vegetable consommé garnished with a sprig of flat-leaf parsley.

BITTER MELON

This vegetable is the size of a cucumber, and has the same ridges and pimples. Bitter melon, like its name, is slightly bitter. But once blanched, sliced in two, and seeded, it absorbs spices and keeps its crunchy texture.

AVAILABILITY:
All year round.

SHOPPING GUIDE:
Select mature melons, slightly soft.

STORAGE:
Will keep for 1 week, loosely wrapped in plastic, in the vegetable drawer of the refrigerator.

Deep-Fried Chinese Noodles with Bitter Melon and Scallops

◆ ◆ ◆

2 bitter melons

½ cup oil, plus more for frying

½ pound tiny bay scallops

Salt and pepper

4 scallions

2-inch piece fresh ginger

1 pound fresh fine Chinese egg noodles*

*These noodles are similar to angel hair pasta (cappellini) and are available in most Oriental food markets.

Boil the bitter melons for 15 minutes. Drain, refresh under cold water, and drain again. Cut each one in half lengthwise. Scrape out the seeds and cut each half across into 1-inch slices. ❖ In a skillet, heat 2 tablespoons of the oil. Add the bitter melon slices and cook over medium heat for 8 minutes. Add the scallops, season with salt and pepper, and cook for 2 more minutes. Remove from the heat and keep warm on top of the stove. ❖ Trim and cut the scallions into 1-inch pieces. Peel and cut the ginger into small pieces. Place the ginger and the scallions in the bowl of a food processor, add 6 tablespoons of the oil, and puree. Transfer to a bowl, season with salt and pepper to taste, and set aside. ❖ Fill a deep-fryer to its capacity with oil and heat to 365 degrees. Drop in the noodles, a handful at a time. After 1 minute, remove them using a slotted spoon and place on paper towels. Continue until you have fried all the noodles. ❖ Place the noodles on a serving platter. Arrange the scallops on top and garnish with the bitter melon slices. Serve with the ginger sauce on the side. ❖ Yield: 4 servings

....

Like angels' hair, deep-fried Chinese noodles form a delicate nest for scallop "pearls" and "bows" of bitter melon. A fragrant ginger sauce accompanies this unusual dish. ▶

CHINESE LONG BEAN

There is nothing mysterious about Chinese long beans. They taste like green beans without strings, and they are really long—from one to three feet. They are sold in bunches of about one pound and come in two colors: light and dark green. I prefer the dark green ones, which are more tender. Cook as you would green beans.

AVAILABILITY:
All year round.

SHOPPING GUIDE:
Select firm, unblemished beans.

STORAGE:
Will keep for at least 1 week, wrapped in plastic, in the vegetable drawer of the refrigerator.

Chinese long beans are sold in tied bunches and taste just like ordinary string beans. Here, they appear with Chinese sausages and elephant garlic, elements of a hearty one-dish meal.

The perfume and pungency of golden fried garlic pervade this plate of steamed long beans and diagonally cut Chinese sausage.

Long Beans with Chinese Sausages

◆ ◆ ◆

2 pounds long beans, trimmed

1 pound Chinese sausage*

¼ cup olive oil

6 cloves garlic, peeled and sliced

3 cups Italian flat-leaf parley sprigs, washed and dried

Salt and pepper

*Chinese sausage is pork-based. It is sold in 1-pound packages of 12. It can be found in Chinese grocery stores.

Cut the long beans across into 4 pieces. Steam for 8 minutes, or until tender. Keep warm in the steamer. ❖ Slice the Chinese sausage across, on the diagonal, into 1-inch pieces. Steam for 8 minutes and keep warm. ❖ In a skillet, heat the oil. When the oil is hot, add the garlic and sauté until golden brown. Drain on paper towels. Fry the parsley sprigs in the hot oil and drain on paper towels. ❖ Combine the beans and the sausage on a platter. Correct the seasoning with salt and pepper and add 2 tablespoons of oil from the pan. Garnish the dish with the fried garlic and parsley and serve. ❖ Yield: 4 servings

....

DAIKON, OR LOH BAAK

I've become a pack rat since I moved away from my mother's house. I visit often, with my husband and babies in tow, to work, to eat, to talk. When we're ready to leave, Colette and I go through a sort of ritual. She combs the pantry and refrigerator for edibles that she might not use in the near future and begs me to take them home. "Experiment," she says. I know what she means, too. It's all for the sake of our careers in the food world, except that she's also reluctant to throw out perfectly good food, and so it goes.

"Experiment," said she, and one day handed me the longest, fattest daikon I had ever seen. It measured about three and one-half feet and weighed what I considered to be a ton. I took the train home that day and was eaten alive by stares from the other passengers. They had the right, I thought. There I was, slightly frazzled from a long day, with a baby in a pouch and a monstrous daikon peeking out from my diaper bag. I would have stared, too.

That night, I served daikon slices with tapenade, dashi with shrimp and daikon, and braised chicken thighs with chunks of daikon, coriander, and ginger. I presented the recipes to my mother the next morning. She said, "Nice. And by the way, I have about three pounds of elephant garlic that I want you to take home. Experiment."

Daikon, or Loh Baak (the Chinese name), is a mild, crisp Oriental radish that is becoming popular in American markets. It is long (usually about a foot), cylindrical, and tapered at the tip. Its flesh is white and covered by a white, very fine skin that you may not even need to peel. Daikon is delicious raw, as a substitute for crackers for dips, in a salad, or grated and used as a bed for all sorts of sauced dishes. It can be added to stews and soups, or pureed with other vegetables. A far cry from the little red radish we are used to, daikon adds flavor, crunch, and depth to many foods.

AVAILABILITY:
All year round; peak season September to January.

SHOPPING GUIDE:
Select firm roots with a nice sheen and skin that is free from soft spots or blemishes. Size matters little.

STORAGE:
Will keep for 2 to 3 days, wrapped in plastic, in the vegetable drawer of the refrigerator.

Daikon, one of the most versatile of Chinese vegetables, is a perfect substitute for radishes. Its bite is pleasant, never harsh.

Braised Daikon with Grapes

• • •

1 large daikon, about 12 inches long and
2 inches in diameter, peeled

2 tablespoons butter

2 tablespoons soy sauce

3/4 cup chicken broth

Salt and pepper

1 pound seedless green grapes

1/2 tablespoon chopped fresh chives or
Chinese or garlic chives

Using a small melon baller, make as many daikon balls as you can. (Add the remaining daikon to a turnip puree or to a soup.) ❖ *In a skillet, melt the butter. Add the daikon balls and sauté for 5 minutes. Add the soy sauce and the chicken broth. Cook for 5 minutes more or until the balls are tender but still crisp. Add salt and pepper to taste and keep warm.* ❖ *Remove the grapes from their stems. Wash and pat dry with paper towels.* ❖ *Using a slotted spoon, transfer the daikon balls to a platter. Add the grapes, mix well, and sprinkle with the chopped chives.* ❖ *Yield: 4 servings*

....

A two-dimensional trompe l'oeil and a three-dimensional taste experience. On a grape serving platter, braised daikon balls with grapes, seasoned with a dash of soy sauce, butter, and chives.

Shredded Daikon with Clams

◆ ◆ ◆

2 dozen littleneck clams

1 large daikon, peeled (12 inches long and 2 inches in diameter)

$\frac{1}{2}$ tablespoon rice vinegar

$\frac{1}{2}$ teaspoon sesame oil

1 tablespoon vegetable oil

Salt and pepper

1 sweet red pepper, seeded and shredded in a food processor

1 cup parsley sauce (see recipe, page 270)

Scrub and rinse the clams. Place the clams in a large saucepan over high heat. Cook, covered, until the clams open. Keep warm. ❖ *Shred the daikon in a food processor fitted with the shredding blade. Place in a large salad bowl.* ❖ *In a small bowl, mix the rice vinegar, oils, and salt and pepper to taste. Pour the sauce over the daikon and toss. Garnish with the red pepper.* ❖ *Using a slotted spoon, remove the clams from the saucepan and arrange around the daikon. Strain the juice through a fine strainer and pour some over the clams. Serve with the parsley sauce.*
❖ Yield: 4 servings

A Japanese wooden box filled with finely shredded daikon, sweet red pepper, and littleneck clams. An almost ephemeral yet distinctive appetizer served with a refreshing parsley sauce.

TARO

We often argue about taro; at least, about its nomenclature. Colette, who favors the Orient in her cuisine, calls it sato imo or woo tau. I've always been partial to South American foods, and call it malanga or yautia. Actually, they are all different yet related varieties of a tropical tuber. For the sake of this book, we've stopped arguing long enough to agree to call them all taro.

Taro can be barrel-shaped and the size of a baking potato, or kidney-shaped and as small as a baby's fist. Both types of taro are "hairy," brown, and have bright white, smooth flesh, marred sometimes by tiny dark specks. Malanga looks more like a hairy yam, has a crisper, yellower flesh, and a more pronounced flavor. Taro (and its cousins) can be boiled, steamed, fried, roasted, added to soups and stews, or enjoyed as a dessert. Large taro roots tend to be drier than small ones; the small ones are less sweet. Choose them small for boiling and steaming, large for baking and for absorbing sauces.

As for its flavor, Colette and I differ on this point as well. She maintains that taro tastes like the marrons *(chestnuts) of her native France; I associate its taste with slightly rancid walnuts. Don't get me wrong...I love taro, especially my mother's fried taro baskets.*

AVAILABILITY:
All year round.

SHOPPING GUIDE:
Select firm, full tubers. Avoid those with shriveled skin or signs of mold.

STORAGE:
Will keep for about 3 days in a basket in a cool, airy place; do not refrigerate.

◄ Two different varieties of taro. Grated taro, like grated potato, can be fried and shaped into "baskets," then filled.

Taro Basket with Red Peppers

◆ ◆ ◆

Our family has known Chef Philip Lee for several years and we dine, *en famille* and with great pleasure, at his New York restaurant. Philip Lee is Hakka—a name that applies to a people and a cuisine originating in northern China. To escape the Mongolian invasion, the Hakka people migrated to Canton and Hong Kong. Although they fostered their own dialect and culture, Hakka cooking took on some elements of Cantonese cuisine, including their way of preparing fish and seafood. Philip Lee introduced us—and New York—to the Hakka way of cooking. Unusual dishes, like small peppers stuffed with fish, roast duck blanketed in taro puree and then deep-fried, and a taro basket filled with seafood. We love his baskets so much that we borrowed the idea and filled ours with—what else?—vegetables.

It's easy to make taro baskets; the secret is having the right tool, a Chinese bird's-nest maker (there's a French version too). It is composed of two metal-mesh bowls with handles. The larger bowl is lined with finely julienned taro and the smaller bowl is inserted. The taro is deep-fried, then released. If you can't get hold of the nest maker, mound some fried julienned taro on a plate, then make an indentation with a small bowl and fill the hollow with the vegetables you wish to serve.

2 pounds taro

Oil for frying

2 cups chicken broth

2 cups fresh or frozen small peas

Rind of 1 lemon

2 large red peppers

4 tablespoons olive oil

Salt and pepper

2 sprigs fresh thyme, leaves only

1 package frozen miniature ears of corn

Parsley leaves for garnish

Peel the taro, then julienne in a food processor fitted with the shredding blade. Wash under cold running water, drain, and spread between several layers of paper towel to dry well. ❖ *Fill a deep-fryer to its capacity with oil and heat to 360 degrees. Lightly oil the bird's-nest maker. Line the bottom and sides with a quarter of the julienned taro. Press the top of the bird's-nest maker down and attach the handles.* ❖ *When the oil is hot, plunge the basket in and cook the taro until golden brown. Remove the basket from the oil, wait about 30 seconds, remove the top, then turn the bowl over and gently tap to release the taro basket. Keep the basket warm until the other 3 baskets are made.* ❖ *Pour the stock into a saucepan. Bring to a boil, add the fresh peas, lower the heat to medium, and cook for 5 minutes, or until tender; drain. (If the peas are frozen, add them to the boiling stock, turn off the heat, and let stand 5 minutes; then drain.)* ❖ *Cut the lemon rind into very thin strips. Cut the red peppers into 1 ½-inch strips. Place the pepper strips on aluminum foil, brush with 2 tablespoons olive oil, and broil for 3 minutes. Sprinkle with salt and pepper and keep warm.* ❖ *In a saucepan, heat the remaining olive oil and add the peas, fresh thyme, and frozen corn. Season with salt and pepper and toss over medium heat until the corn is hot.* ❖ *Fill the baskets with the peas and corn. Garnish with lemon rind and parsley leaves. Serve each basket topped with a few red pepper strips.*
❖ Yield: 4 servings

....

Japanese walking shoes hint at the origins of this spectacular taro dish. Early June peas and miniature corn fill a delicate taro "basket." Lemon zest and thyme flavor these springtime vegetables, while grilled red pepper adds color. ▶

Lemon Stuffed with Taro

* * *

On one of our "mad scientist" days, we were experimenting with taro puree. Spoonful after spoonful was tasted, seasoned, tasted again. And rejected. Then we broke for lunch: sourdough bread, country ham, pears, and Stilton cheese. That was it! We added a bit of Stilton to the taro…heaven on earth! Serve these elegant stuffed lemons with a simple roast chicken.

8 lemons

2 pounds taro

Salt and freshly ground pepper

2 ounces Stilton cheese

3 tablespoons butter

3 cups chicken broth

2 tablespoons sugar

2 tablespoons dark soy sauce

2 sprigs fresh coriander, leaves only,
for garnish

Slice 1 inch off the top of each lemon and a thin slice off the bottom so that the lemons can sit on a plate. Using a grapefruit knife, remove all the flesh from the lemons, leaving a hollow shell. (Use the flesh to make lemonade.) ❖ *Peel and quarter the taro. Place the pieces in a saucepan, cover with water, and add 1 teaspoon salt. Bring to a boil, lower the heat to medium, and cook until tender, about 15 minutes.* ❖ *Drain the taro, reserving ¼ cup of the liquid. Place the taro, the reserved cooking liquid, the cheese, and 1 tablespoon of the butter in the bowl of a food processor and puree. Transfer the puree to a bowl, add salt and pepper to taste, and keep warm.*
Place the lemons and their tops side by side in a saucepan. Add the chicken broth. Bring to a boil, lower the heat to medium, cover, and cook for 15 minutes. Drain. ❖ *In the same saucepan, melt*

the remaining 2 tablespoons butter, add the lemons, sprinkle with sugar and soy sauce, and sauté over medium heat for 5 minutes, or until the lemons are golden brown. ❖ *Using a spatula, transfer the lemons to a serving platter. Fill the lemons with the taro puree. Garnish each with a coriander leaf. Cap the lemons with their tops.* ❖
Yield: 4 servings

The children of invention, these lemons—stuffed with a luscious mixture of Stilton cheese and taro puree—are garnished with radish sprouts and kumquats.

CHINESE CABBAGE

Acabbage, a Western cabbage, that is, held in the hand for testing weight, seems impervious to the elements. Before I met my husband in Paris, I had an Austrian roommate who liked to braise shredded red cabbage in bacon fat and vinegar. It was a good dish, but it became a bad dish since we ate it at least once a week with boiled potatoes dabbed with mustard. In those days I yearned for sushi, clear consommé, meringues—anything to counter those heavy dinners. My roommate prepared oatmeal at seven in the morning and her favorite dessert was a baked apple in pastry topped with crème fraîche. Ever since I left that apartment in the nineteenth arrondissement, cabbage has been virtually banned from my kitchen.

Chinese cabbages are allowed, however. Of the many types available, none is tough or harshly flavored, nor do Chinese cabbages require the long cooking of some of their Western counterparts. My favorite happens to be flowering cabbage, or choy sum, which has a particularly light, mild flavor and pretty yellow buds among its loose, green leaves. When I feel like making a restorative meal, I chop up flowering cabbage and boil it briefly in chicken broth, then add cooked Chinese rice noodles, scallions, and sliced hard-boiled quail eggs. My mother is partial to bok choy and uses it often instead of regular cabbage in winter stews.

Chinese flowering cabbage

Short and long bok choy

Sow cabbage

Shanghai bok choy

Chinese flat cabbage

Bamboo mustard cabbage

Chinese kale

Tientsin cabbage, or Napa cabbage

CHINESE FLOWERING CABBAGE, OR CHOY SUM

Chinese flowering cabbage has green leaves, tiny, bright yellow flowers, and lightly grooved stems about a quarter of an inch in diameter. This cabbage is sold in bunches of five or six stalks.

AVAILABILITY:
All year round, best October to March.

SHOPPING GUIDE:
Select bunches with uniform stems and brightly colored flowers.

STORAGE:
Will keep for 4 to 5 days, in a sealed plastic bag, in the vegetable drawer of the refrigerator.

Chinese Flowering Cabbage Quiche with Water Chestnuts

❖ ❖ ❖

1 recipe pâte brisée (see recipe, page 270)

2 pounds Chinese flowering cabbage

3 eggs

½ cup heavy cream

Salt and pepper

1 pound fresh water chestnuts, peeled, or one 16-ounce can, drained

1 teaspoon sesame oil

3 tablespoons pine nuts

2-inch piece fresh ginger, peeled and minced

Preheat the oven to 325 degrees.
❖ Make the pâte brisée as directed. On a floured board, roll the dough into a circle a little larger than a 9-inch pie pan. Butter and flour the pie pan. Line the pan with the dough, crimp the edges, and prick the bottom. Bake for 15 minutes. Remove from the oven. ❖ Wash and trim the cabbage. Blanch in boiling water, then refresh under cold running water. Drain and pat dry. Coarsely chop the cabbage and set aside. ❖ In a bowl, beat the eggs with the cream and season with salt and pepper to taste. Add the mixture to the cabbage and set aside. ❖ Cook the fresh water chestnuts in boiling water for 6 minutes. Drain. (Do not cook canned water chestnuts.) ❖ In the same saucepan, heat the sesame oil, add the pine nuts, and sauté for 2 minutes. Add the water chestnuts, ginger, and salt and pepper to taste and mix well. Remove from the heat. ❖ Pour the cabbage-egg mixture into the pie crust. Add the water chestnuts and pine nuts. Bake for 25 minutes, or until a toothpick inserted in the center comes out clean.
❖ Yield: 6 servings

Broiled Red Snapper with Chinese Greens

* * *

4 red snappers (about 1 pound each)

Salt and pepper

1-inch piece fresh ginger, peeled and sliced

1 pound broccoli raab

2 eggs

1 teaspoon fresh dill

2 tablespoons sesame oil

1 pound fresh water chestnuts, peeled, or one 16-ounce can, drained

2 pounds any Chinese greens, washed and coarsely chopped

1 tablespoon vegetable oil

1 small sweet red pepper (optional)

1 lemon, cut in wedges

Preheat the oven to 375 degrees.

❖ Wash and pat dry the red snappers. Sprinkle each with salt and pepper, including the cavities. Make 2 incisions on the side of each fish and insert a thin slice of ginger. Set aside. ❖ Steam the broccoli raab for 5 minutes. Transfer to the bowl of a food processor, add the eggs, dill, and salt and pepper to taste, and puree. Stuff each fish with 2 to 3 tablespoons of puree. Drizzle ½ teaspoon of sesame oil on each fish, wrap each tightly in aluminum foil, and bake for 10 minutes. Remove from the oven and keep wrapped in foil. ❖ Boil the fresh water chestnuts for 6 minutes, or until just done. Drain. (Do not cook canned water chestnuts.) ❖ In a large skillet, heat the vegetable oil with the remaining sesame oil. Add the Chinese greens and sauté for 3 minutes. Add the water chestnuts and 3 tablespoons water and cook for another 3 minutes. Adjust the seasoning with salt and pepper to taste and remove from the heat. ❖ Cut the red pepper (if desired) into very thin strips. Add to the greens, mix well but do not cook. ❖ Place 1 fish on each of 4 individual serving plates. Open the foil. Arrange the vegetables around the fish and serve with lemon wedges.

❖ Yield: 4 servings

A broiled red snapper stuffed with pureed broccoli raab and served with sautéed Chinese greens. Red pepper gives a touch of color and dill adorns the gingered fish.

SHORT OR LONG BOK CHOY, OR PEKING CABBAGE

These are often referred to in supermarkets as Chinese cabbage, and are the most popular of the Chinese cabbages. They are compact, barrel-shaped, with white crunchy stalks and crinkled pale green or yellow leaves. This cabbage comes in two sizes: long and narrow (twelve to eighteen inches long and about four inches in diameter) or short (ten to twelve inches and at least six inches in diameter). Use the short one for stuffing and braising, the long one for salad or to shred.

AVAILABILITY:
All year round.

SHOPPING GUIDE:
Select large, compact heads with crisp leaves.

STORAGE:
Will keep for 4 to 5 days, wrapped in plastic, in the vegetable drawer of the refrigerator.

SHANGHAI BOK CHOY

This cabbage is in the same family as the Chinese cabbage, but it is smaller and its leaves are wide and pale green, as are the stalks. Each Shanghai bok choy looks like a large flower with six to seven leaves and is no more than ten inches long.

AVAILABILITY:
All year round.

SHOPPING GUIDE:
Select heads with fresh, crisp leaves with firm stalks. Allow 1 head per serving.

STORAGE:
Will keep for 2 to 3 days, wrapped in plastic, in the vegetable drawer of the refrigerator.

Salad of Long Bok Choy with Blackberries

◆ ◆ ◆

One evening, Marianne came over for dinner all flushed. Leaving the subway, she had passed a man selling luscious-looking blackberries from the back of his truck for "practically nothing…$1.00 a pint!" Pleased at having found a bargain, she bought six pints and triumphantly brought them to us as a gift. Everybody knows that blackberries don't keep. What was I to do with six pints? We ate some with crème fraîche for dinner—Marianne went through a pint of the berries by herself—and the next day, I tossed a few into a salad of bok choy. The result was unusual but very tasty. I served this new salad with thin slices of cold meat loaf, Dijon-style mustard, and a warm onion baguette.

1 long bok choy (about 2 pounds)

2 tablespoons oil

1 tablespoon raspberry vinegar

Salt and pepper

1 tablespoon finely chopped flowering chives or regular chives

1 pint blackberries, washed and drained

Remove the outer leaves of the bok choy. (Use them for soup or chop them for stuffing chicken or fish.) Shred the rest of the cabbage and place in a large salad bowl. ❖ *In a small bowl, mix together the oil, vinegar, and salt and pepper to taste. Add the chives, mix well, and pour over the cabbage. Toss, add the blackberries, and gently toss again.* ❖ Yield: 4 to 6 servings

....

Finely shredded bok choy is seasoned with fragrant raspberry vinaigrette echoed by the flavor of the fresh blackberries that top this refreshing salad. We used sprigs of mint to garnish. ▶

Stuffed Long Bok Choy

◆ ◆ ◆

Marianne loves beer. While she was breast-feeding, and on my recommendation, she drank it every evening with relish. And when she dined at my house, I made sure the meal was one that went well with beer. Japanese stuffed cabbage is one of her favorites. The recipe calls for minced garlic; when I prepared it for Marianne, I left it out, since she claimed that her baby didn't like the taste. Wait till I take little Matthew to Chinatown…without her!

1 long bok choy (about 2 pounds)

1 pound ground pork

1 egg

1 teaspoon sesame oil

1 clove garlic, peeled and minced

1/2 tablespoon chopped chives

Salt and pepper

4 cups chicken broth

Dijon-style mustard

Blanch the cabbage for 5 minutes in boiling water. Drain. Separate the leaves. Cut about 3 inches off the bottom of the white ribs, and coarsely chop them in a food processor. Set aside. ❖ *In a bowl, combine the pork, egg, sesame oil, garlic, chives, and the chopped cabbage. Add salt and pepper to taste.* ❖ *Place 1 heaping teaspoon of pork mixture in the center of a cabbage leaf. Place this leaf on top of another leaf and roll tightly. Secure with a string. Repeat this step until all the stuffing and leaves have been used.* ❖ *In a large saucepan, bring the broth to a boil, lower the heat, and gently add the cabbage rolls. Simmer gently for 30 minutes.* ❖ *Arrange the cabbage rolls on individual serving plates. Remove the strings and serve with Dijon-style mustard.*
❖ Yield: 4 servings

. . . .

Bok choy leaves are stuffed with pork in this Oriental twist on stuffed cabbage. Sesame oil, used to season the meat, marries beautifully with Dijon mustard. Flat-leaf parsley decorates this Japanese earthenware plate.

Steamed Chinese Greens with Pink Mayonnaise

◆ ◆ ◆

This recipe can be prepared with any Chinese greens. It is excellent as an appetizer; also as a light lunch with dry white wine and hot rolls.

2 pounds Chinese cabbage

1 tablespoon butter

1 tablespoon olive oil

2 cloves elephant garlic, peeled and sliced

½ pound medium shrimp, shelled and deveined

Salt and pepper

Paprika

2 serrano chilies, seeded and thinly sliced

1 cup pink mayonnaise (see recipe, page 269)

Wash the cabbage and trim off the stems. Cut each cabbage in half lengthwise. Steam for 5 minutes. Keep warm. ❖ *In a skillet, melt the butter with the oil. Add the sliced garlic and the shrimp. Sauté over medium heat until the garlic is golden brown and the shrimp turn pink, about 4 minutes. Do not overcook. Season with salt and pepper and a pinch of paprika.* ❖ *Arrange the greens on a serving platter. Top with the shrimp and sliced garlic and sprinkle with the sliced hot chilies. Pour some of the cooking fat on top. Serve with the pink mayonnaise on the side.*
❖ Yield: 4 servings

....

▲
Sautéed shrimp and sliced elephant garlic are set amid the leaves of a whole, steamed Chinese flat cabbage; its heart is steamed longer and placed alongside. The pink mayonnaise with sundried tomatoes counterbalances the garlic.

SOW CABBAGE

This cabbage, like bok choy, has long, wide green leaves with smooth edges attached to a central stalk. This cabbage is excellent for stuffing.

AVAILABILITY:
All year round.

SHOPPING GUIDE:
Select heads with firm stems, unblemished leaves, and a compact heart.

STORAGE:
Will keep for 2 to 3 days, wrapped in plastic, in the vegetable drawer of the refrigerator.

CHINESE FLAT CABBAGE

This cabbage is not available everywhere, but if you pass through your city's Chinatown, look for it. It grows flat and round, ten to fourteen inches in diameter, and has small, tender green leaves and white stalks.

AVAILABILITY:
All year round; best October to March.

SHOPPING GUIDE:
Select young heads with tight centers and bright green leaves. Allow 1 head for 2 servings.

STORAGE:
Will keep for 2 to 3 days, wrapped in plastic, in the vegetable drawer of the refrigerator.

BAMBOO MUSTARD CABBAGE

This cabbage's leaves are attached to a long root-like stem. The leaves are pale green with crinkly edges; they look very much like romaine. Bamboo mustard cabbage has a slightly bitter taste; it has to be blanched before cooking. It is excellent in soup and stews and mixed with other greens, and has a spicy taste that contrasts nicely with the sweetness of lamb.

AVAILABILITY:
November to March.

SHOPPING GUIDE:
Select heads with crisp, unblemished leaves and firm stems.

STORAGE:
Will keep for 2 to 3 days, wrapped in plastic, in the vegetable drawer of the refrigerator.

Stuffed Bamboo Mustard Cabbage with Yogurt Sauce

❖ ❖ ❖

1 bunch bamboo mustard cabbage

½ pound ground lamb

½ cup long-grain rice

Salt and pepper

Cumin

Juice of 1 lemon

3 tablespoons oil

2 cloves garlic, peeled and sliced

4 pork chops

1 tablespoon soy sauce

2 cups yogurt

Wash and pat dry the cabbage leaves. Set aside 2 leaves. ❖ *In a bowl, combine the lamb, rice, salt and pepper to taste, a pinch of cumin, and ½ tablespoon lemon juice.* ❖ *Spread the leaves flat. In the center of each leaf, place 1 tablespoon of the stuffing. Fold the top of the leaf up and over the stuffing, fold the sides, and tightly roll the leaf. Repeat until you have used all the stuffing.* ❖ *Line a saucepan with 1 of the reserved leaves. Arrange 2 layers of the stuffed leaves in the saucepan, leaving no gaps between the rolls. Cover with the other reserved leaf. Add 2 cups of water, the remaining lemon juice, and 1 tablespoon oil, cover, and bring to a boil. Lower the heat and simmer for 30 minutes.* ❖ *In a skillet, heat 2 tablespoons of the oil. Add the garlic and sauté for 2 minutes.* *Add the pork chops and cook to desired doneness. Season with salt and pepper to taste and transfer to a platter. Add 3 tablespoons water and the soy sauce to the pan and scrape the skillet.* ❖ *Place the yogurt and the sauce from the pan in the bowl of a food processor and process for 1 minute. Correct the seasoning and pour into a bowl.* ❖ *Arrange the stuffed leaves on a round platter and serve with the pork chops. Serve the yogurt sauce separately.* ❖ *Yield: 4 servings*

▲

Resembling Greek-style stuffed vine leaves, these bundles nestled in an Indian *papadoum* bread are stuffed bamboo mustard cabbage leaves served with a pork chop and a mushroom cap filled with yogurt sauce.

The play of color and texture in this rustic dish befits its lively flavor. Steamed Chinese cabbage is topped with velvety black beans and a peppery onion sauce.

Chopped Chinese Cabbage with Black Beans and Onion Sauce

◆ ◆ ◆

This dish can be made with any green Chinese cabbage. Serve it with steamed basmati rice and ice-cold cider.

2 pounds green Chinese cabbage

3 tablespoons olive oil

½ teaspoon sesame oil

Salt and pepper

One 16-ounce can black beans

1 clove garlic, peeled and minced

1 cup onion sauce (see recipe, page 269)

1 tablespoon chopped fresh coriander

Wash and pat dry the Chinese cabbage. Steam for 3 minutes. Remove from the steamer and coarsely chop. ❖ *In a skillet, heat 1 tablespoon of the olive oil with the sesame oil. Add the cabbage and sauté for 3 minutes. Correct the seasoning with salt and pepper to taste. Set aside and keep warm.* ❖ *Rinse and drain the black beans. In a small saucepan, heat 1 tablespoon of the remaining olive oil, add the garlic, and sauté, stirring, for 1 minute. Add the beans, mix well, and heat gently. Season with salt and pepper to taste.* ❖ *Place the green cabbage on a serving platter. Top with the black beans and the onion sauce. Sprinkle with coriander and serve.* ❖ *Yield: 4 servings*

CHINESE KALE

Chinese kale has wide, pale green leaves, a long smooth stem, and a cluster of white flowers. The leaves have a powerful taste but the stem is tender and sweet.

AVAILABILITY:
All year round.

SHOPPING GUIDE:
Select bunches with unblemished leaves, firm stems with several buds, and fresh-looking flowers.

STORAGE:
Will keep for 2 to 3 days, wrapped in plastic, in the vegetable drawer of the refrigerator.

TIENTSIN CABBAGE, OR NAPA CABBAGE

There are several varieties of this cabbage. They differ in shape and size, according to the season. Tientsin, or Napa, cabbage is easily recognized by its large, white, crunchy stalks and short green leaves.

AVAILABILITY:
All year round.

SHOPPING GUIDE:
Select crisp-looking heads with unblemished leaves. Smaller cabbages have tenderer leaves, especially in summer.

STORAGE:
Will keep for 4 to 5 days, in a plastic bag, in the vegetable drawer of the refrigerator.

Youth is an important factor in choosing Chinese vegetables at the market. Chinese kale can be bitter when old; here, young, fresh leaves of Chinese kale are coupled with stem ginger, the newest spring growth of this pungent seasoning.

SQUASH

SUMMER SQUASH

When I was in the fourth grade, I had a singular passion for the American Indian. My first report ever was about the Iroquois and I learned, at the age of nine, that this Eastern tribe ate maize, beans, and lots of asquutasquash, or what we have abbreviated to squash. I have since given up my desire to become an American Indian but I still favor squash, and agree with a Mr. Williams who wrote, in his tome Key to the Indian Language, circa 1643, that squashes were "sweet, light, wholesome and refreshing." They are also easy to prepare. I should know because my baby son, Matthew, liked pureed squash more than peas, carrots, and ice cream combined. Depending on the season, I'd just cut up a Table Queen (acorn type), crookneck, turban, or zucchini, steam it, and puree it with a touch of butter. His grandmother is against baby food in jars.

Warm-weather cucurbits share a tenderness and fragility that defy heavy sauces or complex seasonings. I like them lightly steamed, drizzled with olive oil, and sprinkled with fresh herbs. In America, say about two decades ago, summer squash was often sold overgrown. Fibrous, thick-skinned, and heavy, these monsters were only fit to be fried, stuffed, or added to a ratatouille. My mother, revolutionary that she is, scoffed at these squashes while others took pride in their weight and size. When she visited her friends at their country homes, she would volunteer to do the garden picking, shocking the hostess by leaving the heavies and picking the babies. She was always forgiven at dinner when she brought a dish of sweet, herbed whole squash to the table.

Now, immigrating Italian chefs have brought with them zucchini in its prime, the way it should be, complete with flowers and an adorable fuzz that indicates youth. Mille grazie.

Zucchini

Chayote

Pattypan

◄ Summer squash—namely, green and yellow zucchini—at an outdoor market. Paired together, steamed, buttered, and herbed, they translate into the best the summer has to offer.

ZUCCHINI

Born in the late fifties, I was too young for sock hops and beat-poetry readings, war demonstrations, the birth of rock 'n' roll. I almost missed the hippie years, too, being a rather serious high school student preoccupied with poetry and the boys in my art class. I was hippyish, though, and wore a red and black peasant skirt from Hungary and hoop earrings almost every day for an entire year, much to my mother's consternation. She shouldn't have been so shocked, really. She, too, was touched—albeit ever so lightly—by hippiedom. Wrapping a red bandana around her head on occasion, and wearing a caftan, she would sometimes visit a friend's loft and listen to a Pakistani intone songs in a minor key accompanied by a sitar.

The vegetable of the day was zucchini. Surely because it was easy to grow, country hippies and commune hippies, even suburban hippies, planted zucchini in their gardens, picked it overgrown, and used it in every facet of their cooking. To excess, in my modest opinion, and I am a zucchini-lover. They'd dole out zucchini omelets, zucchini pancakes, stuffed zucchini, zucchini pasta sauce, zucchini stir-fry (a favorite among my hippie high school friends), and, of course, the culinary badge of the hippiest hippies, zucchini bread. So did I—or my mother—tire of the dark green, sweet-fleshed squash? Not a bit. We simply came up with new and better recipes, wowing our friends with our innovations. We made velvety zucchini soup and light-as-air fritters, but we really caused a revolution when we chose finger-sized zucchini, steamed them whole and sprinkled them with chopped fresh savory and a tiny bit of mint. That must have been the beginning of the end of the hippie movement.

AVAILABILITY:
All year round.

SHOPPING GUIDE:
Select small zucchini with shiny skin. Avoid dried-out blossom ends.

STORAGE:
Will keep for 3 to 4 days, wrapped in plastic, in the vegetable drawer of the refrigerator.

Only quite recently have squash flowers been favored by American cooks. Seen here, innocently peeking from squash plants, zucchini flowers can be steamed, stuffed, braised, or simply left attached as a sweet reminder of nature's tenor.

CHAYOTE, OR MIRLITON

I was combing the markets of New York's Spanish Harlem with Marianne when I first laid eyes on a chayote. There it was, pale green and pear shaped, with skin as smooth as a baby's bottom. We bought three and wondered aloud how to cook them. We asked a woman who was shopping at the bodega. She stared at us blankly, then smiled and said, "No English." Both Marianne and I know a smattering of Spanish (after all, it's the second official language of New York City), so we blurted out the same question in what we thought was her native tongue. She answered, once again, "No English." Now we were truly confused. With the help of the bodega owner, we came to understand that she was French and lived in Martinique, where chayotes are abundant! The chattering, this time in fluent French on all sides, astounded the bodega owner, who shooed us out after a few minutes.

From Hélène Le Caibaud, we learned that we could steam them and add any sauce we wished, since chayote has a pleasant, mild flavor. She also told us that Napoleon had them imported from Martinique when he realized that Josephine was not interested in him. She was so grateful for the gift—she adored *chayottes*—that she finally gave her heart and hand to the Emperor.

The pear-shaped chayote has a creased, pale green rind and one soft seed at its center. It grows on thick, twisted vines in Florida, California, and the Caribbean. It can be boiled, fried, added to soups, sautéed with other vegetables, served as a salad, or stuffed.

Chayotes are the squash of choice among immigrants who hail from the Caribbean. We have gleefully adopted this mild-flavored vegetable, since it takes well to some of our more adventurous and unusual sauces.

AVAILABILITY:
All year round; best September to December.

SHOPPING GUIDE:
Select small chayotes, about 6 inches long and weighing no more than ¼ pound, with smooth skin. Avoid those with blemishes or brown or soft spots.

STORAGE:
Will keep for 3 to 4 days, wrapped in plastic, in the vegetable drawer of the refrigerator.

Chayote Salad with Baby Shrimp

❖ ❖ ❖

2 chayotes

1 ounce dried shredded seaweed, soaked in
lukewarm water for 20 minutes*

4 leaves radicchio

1 tablespoon lemon juice

4 tablespoons olive oil

2 cloves garlic, peeled and minced

Salt and pepper

1 ounce baby shrimp, cooked

2 sprigs fresh dill

1 lemon, cut in wedges

*Available in 2-ounce packages in Oriental grocery stores.

*Cut the chayotes across into ¼ inch slices. Remove
the pits. Steam or boil the chayote slices, uncovered, for 15 minutes, or until tender when pierced
with a fork. Drain and keep at room temperature.*
❖ *Drain the seaweed and place in a salad bowl.*
❖ *Wash the radicchio leaves and pat dry.* ❖
*In a small bowl, mix together the lemon juice and
3 tablespoons of the olive oil. Add the garlic and
salt and pepper to taste. Pour the sauce over the
seaweed and toss.* ❖ *Arrange 1 radicchio leaf
on each of 4 individual serving plates. Top each leaf
with some seaweed salad and arrange several
chayote slices over the seaweed. Brush the slices
with the remaining olive oil and arrange several tiny
shrimp on top. Garnish with dill and lemon wedges.*
❖ *Yield: 4 servings*

On a hot summer's day, what could be more
pleasing than a salad of silky chayote, baby shrimp,
Chinese seaweed, and radicchio? The seaweed is
tossed in a garlicky, lemony vinaigrette.

Bubbly-hot and inviting, a gratin of chayote is seasoned with serrano chilies and onions and garnished with a sprig of mint.

Chayote au Gratin

• • •

4 chayotes

2 tablespoons butter

Salt

5 green serrano chilies, seeded and coarsely chopped

2 large onions, peeled and thinly sliced

¼ pound Swiss or gruyère cheese, sliced

1 egg

¼ cup milk

½ cup heavy cream

2 tablespoons chopped fresh chives

Preheat the oven to 375 degrees ❖
Thinly slice the unpeeled chayotes across. Place the slices in a large saucepan and cover with boiling water. Cook over medium heat, uncovered, for 15 minutes, or until barely done. ❖ *Butter a 1 ½ - quart gratin dish with 1 tablespoon of the butter. Cover the bottom with a layer of chayote and sprinkle with salt and some of the chilies. Add a layer of sliced onions, then a layer of cheese. Continue layering until all ingredients are used, finishing with cheese.* ❖ *In a bowl, beat the egg with the milk and cream. Pour the mixture over the layered chayote. Dot with the remaining butter. Bake for 25 minutes, or until the top is golden brown.* ❖ *Just before serving, sprinkle with chopped chives.* ❖ *Yield: 6 servings*

PATTYPAN SQUASH

Whenever I see pattypan squash in a market, I'm immediately reminded of an old-fashioned French china plate by the squash's delicate scalloped edges and its pale—almost translucent—green color. Of all the summer squashes, pattypans are probably the least flavorful. They are usually too watery when simply steamed or baked; however, they are delicious as a container for stuffings. Imagine leftover pot roast or chicken, chopped and mixed with celery and red peppers, then stuffed in this lovely green scalloped dish. In July, when tomatoes are at their best, I fill steamed, cooled pattypan with peeled, chopped tomatoes bound by a light lemony mayonnaise. I always find myself dreaming of colors when I prepare pattypan.

AVAILABILITY:
May to September.

SHOPPING GUIDE:
Select small squash that is firm to the touch. Avoid those with bruises.

STORAGE:
Will keep for 1 to 2 days, wrapped in plastic, in the vegetable drawer of the refrigerator.

A caring grower suggests—on his sign—some of the many ways to prepare spring's harbinger: squash blossoms. Our own favorite method is to steam gently and drizzle with fruity olive oil. ▶

Vegetable Bouillabaisse

• • •

5 strands saffron, soaked in 1 cup hot water for 1 hour

2 quarts fish stock

3 carrots, peeled and cut into 2-inch pieces

3 kohlrabi, peeled, sliced, and quartered

6 baby chayotes, sliced*

6 baby turnips, peeled*

4 parsnips, peeled and cut into 2-inch pieces

2 yellow peppers, seeded and cut into 1-inch strips

2 green peppers, seeded and cut into 1-inch strips

3 cloves garlic, peeled and crushed

pound snow peas, strings removed

12 cherry tomatoes, cut in half and seeded

Salt and pepper

12 slices French baguette, toasted

¼ cup *rouille* (see recipe, page 270) or 1 4-ounce jar *harissa* sauce (available in specialty stores)

*If baby chayotes or baby turnips are not available, replace them with 1 chayote, peeled, sliced, and pit removed and 3 turnips, peeled and quartered.

Strain the saffron over a bowl, reserving the liquid. ❖ *In a large saucepan, heat the fish stock. Add the saffron water and all the vegetables except the snow peas and the tomatoes. Bring to a boil, lower the heat, and simmer for 15 minutes. The vegetables should be barely tender. Add the snow peas and tomatoes and cook for 2 minutes. Season with salt and pepper to taste.* ❖ *Spread the* rouille *or harissa* thinly on the baguette slices. ❖ *Serve the soup along with the toast.* ❖ *Yield: 6 servings*

Squash
Blossoms
375/½ lb

Batter Dipr-fry
Sauté
Eat in salads
Stuff & Bake

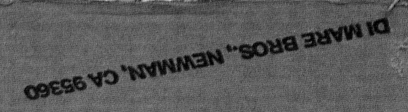

DI MARE BROS., NEWMAN, CA 95360

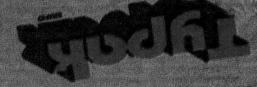

TOMATOES

WINTER SQUASH

On the off chance that a winter squash turns up on your table, you should know that you made an excellent decision. We imagine you at the supermarket on a November evening, eyes riveted to the enormous pile of gourd-like prehistoric-looking protuberances, trying very hard to remember when you last cooked one. The green beans are quite sad this time of year, but at least they're familiar and—small. And the carrots in plastic have a comfortable look; you could always puree them with a potato or two. Your hands reach for the carrots. We are whispering in your ear, now and forever: "Pick the squash and you will not regret it."

Winter squash is the most versatile vegetable under gray skies, and the most beautiful. It has all the strength and nobility of spirit of the American Indian, who began to cultivate it more than two thousand years ago, long before explorers introduced it to Europe in the sixteenth century. Like the legendary Indian chiefs, each of the many squash varieties is painted in a distinct color: fiery orange, forest green, citrine yellow, gentle white. The skin of the winter squash is most often thick and glossy, useful as a cooking vessel for all manner of savory stuffings. Its tender, nutty-sweet flesh blends perfectly with both sweetenings and herbs. Finally, like the wise medicine man, the winter squash has an ancient look, formed by the earth and, at times, weathered by the elements. That is why both of us revere these sturdy, mellow vegetables.

In the last two decades, however, an interesting phenomenon concerning the noble squash has caught our attention. The Japanese have developed several new varieties that not only show off squash's best qualities—sweetness and adaptability—but also bring new colors, shapes, and textures

Winter squash

Delicata squash

Sweet dumpling

Kabocha

Jack-Be-Little

Spaghetti squash

Hokkaido

◄ The variety of winter squashes is, as evidenced in this still life, astounding. First row, left to right: acorn, sweet dumpling. Second row: Hokkaido, cut-open spaghetti squash, golden nugget. Third row: whole spaghetti squash, delicata. Bottom row: Jack-Be-Littles, kabocha.

to our supermarket shelves. These include the Hokkaido, the delicata, and the sweet dumpling, all of which are now grown in the United States. Our excitement at these newcomers has produced some of our most innovative recipes.

When the Greenmarket, a program of the Council on the Environment of New York City, opened on New York's Union Square in 1976, I immediately got into the habit of going shopping there every Saturday. I'd buy fruit and vegetables for the week, meet my friends, exchange recipes, and, when the occasion arose, introduce them to new varieties of vegetables that I had noticed at the stands. I wondered, that first year, if my Saturday morning outing would end at the first frost. What would the farmers sell? I asked Jessica Vecchione, a young woman who works at Windfall Farms in Montgomery, New York. "Squash," she replied. "All sorts of winter squash."

Of course! I had forgotten about winter squash: the acorn, the hubbard, the butternut, and one of Marianne's favorites, the spaghetti squash. Jessica began her professional life in advertising but when she inherited a parcel of land, she decided to get off the fast lane and become an organic farmer. Morse Pitts, owner of Windfall Farms, asked her to join him and she now grows and sells produce with verve and intelligence.

Morse and Jessica and their crew grow smaller-than-usual, tender butternut squash, a super-sweet, two-tone acorn squash, and brilliant orange Jack-Be-Littles. Jessica introduced me to her acorn squash, explaining that the usual way to bake it—that is, with butter and honey—didn't do justice to its flavor. She told me to fill its cavity with a mixture of a beaten egg, fresh goat cheese, and pink peppercorns before popping it in the oven at 375 degrees for forty minutes. I wouldn't eat it any other way.

DELICATA SQUASH

The delicata is, in our opinion, one of the most interesting and adaptable squashes. It is oblong in shape (like a fat cucumber) and measures about ten to twelve inches long. Distinctive both because of its coloring (bright yellow with dark orange stripes) and its taste—delicate, hence its name, with a slightly sweet, corn-like flavor. Its flesh is not dense, like other squashes, and it therefore has a characteristic lightness, blending well with other foods. It is perfect for stuffing.

AVAILABILITY:
October to February.

SHOPPING GUIDE:
Select squash with deep-orange stripes, which indicate full maturity. Avoid mushiness and bruises.

STORAGE:
Will keep for up to 1 month, unwrapped, in a cool, airy place.

Delicata squash, here stuffed with a veal and herb mixture and graced with an edible pansy, brings drama to oft-drab winter.

Delicata Squash with Veal

◆ ◆ ◆

2 delicata squash

½ pound ground veal

1 garlic clove, minced

1 teaspoon dried thyme

1 teaspoon sesame oil

1 large egg

Salt and pepper

6 hard-boiled quail eggs (optional)

2 cups chicken stock

6 sprigs cilantro

Preheat oven to 350°.

❖ *Cut a ½-inch slice from both ends of each squash. With a narrow, long-handled spoon (an iced-tea spoon is ideal), gently scoop out the seeds. Set aside.* ❖ *In a bowl, mix together the veal, garlic, thyme, sesame oil, and egg. Add salt and pepper to taste.* ❖ *Peel the quail eggs. Divide the meat into two equal portions.* ❖ *Using the spoon, push a walnut-sized portion of meat into the squash, then insert a quail egg, followed by more meat. Repeat this step until you have used 3 quail eggs per squash. Seal the edges with aluminum foil. Arrange squash in a baking pan. Pour in the stock and bake for 35 minutes, or until a fork easily pricks the skin.* ❖ *Slice the squash into rounds about 1 inch thick. Garnish each slice with a small cilantro leaf.* ❖ *Yield: 4 servings*

SWEET DUMPLING

Born in Japan only twenty years ago and now available in the United States, this lovely, small squash is perfect to serve for a tête-à-tête dinner. About four inches in diameter and plump, the sweet dumpling has a pale yellow, starchy flesh with a honey-blessed taste that will satisfy two people. Its skin is cream-colored or yellowish with green stripes.

AVAILABILITY:
September to December.

SHOPPING GUIDE:
Select squash that is heavy for its size with green stripes. Avoid green-tinged skin, mottling, and soft spots.

STORAGE:
Will keep for only 10 days, unwrapped, in a cool, airy place.

KABOCHA

Our absolute favorite winter squash, kabocha has a fine, rich, sweet flavor and a tender, potato-like flesh when cooked. An average kabocha weighs about three pounds and is pumpkin- or turban-shaped, with dark green mottled skin. It is excellent pureed, baked, steamed, or stuffed. Try using this new squash in desserts instead of pumpkin or sweet potato.

AVAILABILITY:
All year round.

SHOPPING GUIDE:
Select squash with the stem intact and fresh-looking. Avoid softness or pitting.

STORAGE:
Will keep for 1 month, unwrapped, in a cool, airy place.

JACK-BE-LITTLE

Halloween was always a nightmare for me. Every time I tried to carve a pumpkin for the children, I either cut myself or mutilated the pumpkin. Never—absolutely never—did I succeed in making a grand, smiling, eerie jack-o'-lantern. As Thanksgiving neared, I would rush to buy canned pumpkin to avoid having to peel and cook one of those monsters. Finally, Jack-Be-Little squash appeared on the market. Small, fluted, and lovely to look at (piled high in a ceramic bowl or old-fashioned basket, they make a harvest-like centerpiece for a fall table), Jack-Be-Littles are delicious baked, or filled with broccoli puree, or as individual "bowls" containing smooth, rich pumpkin soup. In any case, their arrival on the market rid me of my pumpkin-phobia!

Jack-Be-Littles are round, bright orange, and usually come with the stems still attached. Slice two inches off the top and scoop out the seeds with a teaspoon. The squash can be baked with butter, stuffed, steamed, or pureed.

AVAILABILITY:
October to January.

SHOPPING GUIDE:
Select firm squash. Avoid those with brown spots.

STORAGE:
Will keep for several weeks, unwrapped, in a cool, airy place.

Jack-Be-Little Soufflé with Pistachios

• • •

Prepare this dish as an appetizer, serving one small squash per person, or as the main course for brunch or lunch with a Belgian endive salad and a good bottle of California Zinfandel.

4 Jack-Be-Little squash

2 cups cooked broccoli, chopped

2 egg yolks

1-inch piece fresh ginger, minced

1 cup shelled pistachios

4 egg whites

Salt and pepper

Preheat the oven to 325 degrees.
❖ *Cut a 1-inch slice from the stem end of each Jack-Be-Little. Set the tops aside. Using a tablespoon, scoop out and discard the seeds. Arrange the squash cut side down, on a baking sheet, along with the tops, and bake for 20 minutes. Remove from the oven and set aside.* ❖ *Place the broccoli, egg yolks, ginger, and half the pistachios in the bowl of a food processor and puree. Season with salt and pepper to taste. Transfer to a bowl.* ❖ *Beat the egg whites with a pinch of salt until stiff. Fold the egg whites into the broccoli puree. Fill each squash with the broccoli mixture.* ❖ *Slice the remaining pistachios with a sharp paring knife. Top each soufflé with a few sliced pistachios. Bake for 30 minutes.* ❖ *Arrange on 4 individual serving plates with the tops on and surround with the remaining sliced pistachios.*
❖ *Yield: 4 servings*

....

Pistachios add an unusual, nutty flavor to the airy broccoli soufflé that blends well with the sweetness of the Jack-Be-Little squash. White wine or beer makes a good partner to this colorful dish. ▶

SPAGHETTI SQUASH

When we first began eating this vegetable, it was as if one of my biggest wishes had been granted. A nonstarchy spaghetti! I could eat tons of it and not get fat. This large (up to twelve inches long), pale yellow squash has a flesh that, when cooked and scraped, forms translucent, spaghetti-like strands with a mild taste. It's the sauce that makes this vegetable come alive; pesto, tomatoes and basil, olives and hot pepper flakes, béchamel, you name it. I prefer halving and boiling this versatile squash; Colette usually bakes it.

AVAILABILITY:
All year round; best September to February.

SHOPPING GUIDE:
Select smooth-skinned squash; the larger the squash, the thicker the strands. Avoid those with soft spots or ridges.

STORAGE:
Will keep for up to 1 month, unwrapped, in a cool, airy place.

A tasty trompe l'oeil. Spaghetti squash, crunchier and more wholesome than pasta, is topped with a faux "tomato" sauce of cranberries and ginger. The fruit sauce is also perfect on the accompanying squab or any broiled poultry. ▶

Squab and Spaghetti Squash with Cranberries

◆ ◆ ◆

4 squabs, split along the backbone

1 tablespoon soy sauce

Juice of ½ lemon

2 tablespoons olive oil

Salt and pepper

1 medium spaghetti squash

2 tablespoons butter

1 heaping tablespoon finely chopped fresh ginger

1 heaping tablespoon finely chopped shallots

1 12-ounce package fresh cranberries

3 tablespoons sugar

Place the squabs in a large bowl. Mix together the soy sauce, lemon juice, and olive oil. Add freshly ground pepper. Pour the sauce over the squabs and marinate for 1 hour. ❖ *Cut the spaghetti squash in half lengthwise, scoop out and discard the seeds. Place the squash in a large saucepan, add water to cover, cover the pan, and bring to a boil. Lower the heat to medium. Cook until tender, about 20 minutes.* ❖ *Melt the butter in a large saucepan. Add the ginger and shallots and sauté briefly over medium heat until softened. Add the cranberries, 1 cup of water, and the sugar. Bring the mixture to a boil, season with salt and pepper to taste, and cook, stirring occasionally, until thick. Taste and correct the seasoning: the sauce should not be sweet.* ❖ *Preheat the broiler for 5 minutes. Broil the squabs for 8 minutes on each side. Keep warm.* ❖ *Drain the squash and remove the flesh by running the tines of a fork along the inside of the squash so that spaghetti-like strands form. Transfer the vegetable spaghetti to one side of a large, shallow serving platter and nap with the sauce. Place the squabs at the other end and serve.* ❖ *Yield: 4 servings*

HOKKAIDO

When I found out that a new Japanese supermarket had opened in Edgewater, New Jersey, on the banks of the Hudson River, I was ecstatic. I dreamed of all the glorious Oriental meals I would create. I would be able to buy fresh soba (buckwheat noodles), pickles, soup bases, and fresh vegetables flown in from Japan. When I got there, I was surprised to see that most of the vegetables were grown in New Jersey. Among the locally grown produce was the prized Japanese winter squash called Hokkaido. In Japan, it is used as the base for a sweet flan or baked with miso sauce. I was told that the New Jersey Hokkaido was even better than its Oriental brother.

Hokkaido looks very much like a turban squash. Its dark green skin hides a pale orange flesh that, when cooked, has a sweet, yam-like flavor. Because of its sweetness, it can easily be used in dessert recipes without the addition of a lot of sugar.

AVAILABILITY:
October to February.

SHOPPING GUIDE:
Select medium, firm squash with glossy skin.

STORAGE:
Will keep for 2 weeks, unwrapped, in a cool, airy place.

Iced Hokkaido Soufflé

◆ ◆ ◆

1 Hokkaido squash

3 egg yolks

1/3 cup sugar

1 1/4 cups heavy cream, whipped

2 tablespoons bourbon

2 egg whites

Quarter the Hokkaido and peel. Scrape away the seeds with a tablespoon and cut each quarter into several pieces. Place the squash pieces in a saucepan and cover with water. Bring to a boil, lower the heat, and simmer for 20 minutes, or until tender. Drain. Puree the squash in a food processor and set aside. ❖ Beat the egg yolks with the sugar in the top portion of a double boiler over simmering water until thick and light in color. Remove from the heat and continue to beat until cooled. Carefully fold in the whipped cream, bourbon, and pureed Hokkaido. Beat the egg whites until stiff and lightly fold into cream mixture. ❖ Gently transfer the mixture into a 2 1/2 -quart mold or springform pan. Cover with wax paper and freeze until firm. ❖ When ready to serve, allow about 15 to 20 minutes of softening at room temperature, then unmold the soufflé onto a round serving platter. ❖ Yield: 4 servings

▲
Many types of squash can be used in desserts. Here, Hokkaido squash is transformed into an iced soufflé, made even richer with the addition of cream and bourbon.

BEANS

In high school, I held the dubious position of being the child of the French teacher. One year, I was even her student. In retrospect, I seem to have taken the matter in stride; I unabashedly called her Mom in class and argued with her stridently as if I had been at home. She, too, played the game with panache. I can only thank the stars that I was proficient in French; I am sure she wouldn't have hesitated—would she have enjoyed?— slapping me with an occasional C minus! One of her golden rules stuck with me ever since, for it had to do with a much-loved vegetable: beans. The French word for bean is haricot, *beginning with an aspirated* h *(a misleading term: it actually signifies a guttural stop without a breath). One day, she came to class with a casserole of green beans cooked with bacon, veal stock, butter, and parsley. We were allowed a portion of the fragrant dish only after correctly indicating whether a particular word had an aspirated or nonaspirated* h. *Her ruse worked and we regaled ourselves with* haricots verts à la bonne femme.

Cranberry bean

Pigeon pea

Green bean

Winged bean

Fava bean

◄ Two vegetables best served raw: spicy French breakfast radishes and the beautiful purple string bean, which loses some of its color when cooked.

CRANBERRY BEAN

The cranberry bean, creamy white and flecked with scarlet, is a type of small flageolet. Only its seeds, flecked with scarlet as well, are eaten.

AVAILABILITY:
July to October.

SHOPPING GUIDE:
Select firm, plump, brightly colored beans. Avoid shriveled ends.

STORAGE:
Will keep 2 to 3 days, wrapped in plastic, in the vegetable drawer of the refrigerator.

Fresh Cranberry Beans with Duck Sausage

◆ ◆ ◆

Ariane Daguin is Amazonian in stature; certainly the tallest French woman we know. Ariane's other important attribute is her skill as a *charcutière*. Her pâtés are famous, her foie gras the best in the United States, and her duck sausage is otherworldly! One day, she served us her duck sausage with fresh braised cranberry beans. We have reproduced our own version here. However, be warned—this dish should be served only: (a) when you're not on a diet or (b) when you really want to impress someone special!

3 tablespoons butter

8 3-ounce duck sausages

Salt and pepper

2 cups (about 2 pounds in the pod) shelled fresh cranberry beans

3 thick slices smoked bacon, cubed

2 tablespoons chopped fresh parsley

In a skillet, melt the butter. Prick the sausages with a fork, put them in the skillet, and cook gently over low heat for 20 minutes, turning often. ❖ *Bring 1 quart of water to a boil. Add ¹/₂ teaspoon salt and the beans. Bring to a boil again, lower the heat to medium, and cook for 10 minutes, or until the beans are tender. Drain.* ❖ *In a heavy skillet, cook the bacon until crisp. Using a slotted spoon, transfer to paper towels.* ❖ *Place the beans in a deep serving platter, add 2 tablespoons bacon fat, the bacon, parsley, and pepper to taste. Toss well and correct the seasoning.* ❖ *Arrange the duck sausages on top of the beans and serve.* ❖ Yield: 4 servings

Inspired by the heavier French *cassoulet,* this dish of small, tender cranberry beans is seasoned with smoked bacon and fresh parsley and served with duck sausage. ▶

Roast Duck with Cranberry Beans

◆ ◆ ◆

1 duck, about 3 to 4 pounds

3 cloves garlic, peeled

1 tablespoon soy sauce

Salt and pepper

2 cups chicken broth

2 cups (about 2 pounds in the pod) shelled
fresh cranberry beans

4 serrano chilies, seeded and sliced

1 bunch radishes (8), sliced

Preheat the oven to 375 degrees.
❖ *Remove as much fat as you can from the duck's
cavity. Prick the duck skin all over with a fork and
pierce through the skin in several places with the
tip of a sharp knife.* ❖ *Cut the garlic into slivers
and insert below the skin. Rub the duck inside and
out with soy sauce. Sprinkle with salt and pepper.*
❖ *Place the duck in a roasting pan, add the
chicken broth, and bake for 1 hour 15 minutes,
basting frequently. Remove from the oven and let
stand on top of the stove until ready to serve. Pour
the pan drippings into a bowl and skim off the layer
of fat with a spoon.* ❖ *Meanwhile, bring 2 quarts
of salted water to a boil. Add the cranberry beans
and cook for 20 minutes, or until tender. Drain.* ❖
*Place the beans in a bowl, add 3 to 4 tablespoons
of duck pan drippings and the chilies, and toss.
Correct the seasoning.* ❖ *Cut the duck into 4
individual serving pieces. Arrange on top of the
beans and garnish with sliced radish. Reheat the
pan drippings and serve separately.*
❖ Yield: 4 servings

....

This bean dish—fresh cranberry beans enlivened
by green chilies, sliced radish, and pan drippings—
accompanies the classic, rich taste of roast duck.

PIGEON PEA

Pigeon peas are small and round. An off-white color, they are usually sold dried in the imported-foods section of supermarkets. Fresh, they have the same color but retain more of their delicious nutty taste. They grow in the South and in the Caribbean. Like lima beans, they are starting to appear in the open markets in the summer and fall.

AVAILABILITY:
March to September.

SHOPPING GUIDE:
Select velvety, smooth-skinned beans with even, bright color that are small for their type. Avoid shriveled or pale-colored beans and ones with brown spots.

STORAGE:
Will keep for up to 2 days, wrapped in plastic, in the vegetable drawer of the refrigerator.

A recent arrival to the markets in its fresh state, the pigeon pea is nutty, slightly starchy, and a delicious alternative to the lima in rich sauces or stews.

GREEN BEAN

Now that I have tasted true French green beans, the American version pales in comparison. French haricots verts (the best are called Fins de Bagnols) are long and as thin as an electrical cord, with a delicate, slightly grassy, succulent flavor. Both my French teacher and I are happy to announce their arrival to the United States. We like to presteam the haricots before gently sautéing them in sweet butter, garlic, and parsley. If you can't find Gallic beans, then look to the Orient. Chinese long (or yard-long) beans (see page 124) are available in all Oriental produce markets and, although considerably longer, share the French bean's elegant thinness and flavor.

When you tire of green, try the burgundy bean. But beware: once cooked, it loses its purple color and resembles an ordinary green bean. Also, there's the yellow wax bean, which I like to cook together with American green beans.

AVAILABILITY:
All year round; best from July to September.

SHOPPING GUIDE:
Select firm, brightly colored beans that snap in half easily.

STORAGE:
Will keep 2 to 3 days, wrapped in plastic, in the vegetable drawer of the refrigerator.

Our familiar string bean, at the bottom of the photo, is hardier, firmer, and crunchier than its French cousin. *Haricots verts*—thin, elegant, and tender—are packed with the utmost care, since they are highly prized in France and the U.S.

Haricots Verts with Chicken Wings

❖ ❖ ❖

8 chicken wings

1 clove garlic, peeled

2 tablespoons soy sauce

Salt and pepper

½ cup chicken broth

1 pound *haricots verts*

2 tablespoons butter

1 tablespoon chopped fresh parsley

2 small, round persimmons,
peeled and sliced

Preheat the oven to 375 degrees.
❖ *Rub the chicken wings with the garlic. Arrange in a baking dish, brush with soy sauce, and sprinkle with freshly ground pepper to taste. Add the chicken broth and bake for 25 minutes, or until golden brown.* ❖ *Bring 1 ½ quarts of water to a boil. Add the* haricots verts, *bring to a boil, lower the heat, and cook for 6 minutes, or until barely tender. Drain.* ❖ *In the same saucepan, melt the butter and add the parsley and salt and pepper to taste. Cook for a few seconds, then add the* haricots verts *and sauté for 2 minutes.* ❖ *Arrange 2 chicken wings on each of 4 individual serving plates. With the* haricots verts, *make a fan opposite the wings, arranging the persimmon slices in the center of each plate.* ❖ *Yield: 4 servings*

....

A delicate fan is formed by pencil-thin *haricots verts* in this pristine dish of roasted chicken wings. Sliced Japanese persimmon and walnuts add a note of sweetness.

WINGED BEAN

The winged bean is a newcomer to the United States. Introduced into this country from New Guinea, Thailand, Vietnam, and the Philippines, the winged bean is tasty and very beautiful. Consisting of a stem and four delicate fins, it can be cut across into fanciful stars and stir-fried, braised, or blanched and tossed into salads. Its flavor is not as grassy as a regular green bean; with more starch and substance, it stands up to rich sauces.

I discovered the winged bean five years ago when I first met Robert Baterna. Robert is a first-generation immigrant from the Philippines who, with his wife, Susan, runs a farm of about thirteen acres in Homestead, Florida. They were cultivating white and green chayote and a vegetable I had never seen before: winged beans. Robert showed me wild-looking vines bearing six- to nine-inch winged beans, dark green and ridged, and said they were beautiful when cut because each slice looks like a star. Robert handed me a bag of beans and invited me to experiment.

Back in New York, I tried them steamed, stir-fried, and sautéed with garlic and parsley. These beans, with their delicate texture and taste, were superb. Unfortunately, during the following five years, it was nearly impossible to find them in produce markets, since they are difficult to pack, the crops grow unevenly, and public demand was not high. But this year Robert and some other farmers in Florida have managed to overcome all these problems, and winged beans are here to stay.

AVAILABILITY:
Early summer.

SHOPPING GUIDE:
Select fresh, dark green winged beans. Avoid limp beans.

STORAGE:
Will keep for 4 to 5 days, in a sealed plastic bag, in the vegetable drawer of the refrigerator.

A sharp knife is the perfect tool for the noble Oriental winged bean. It can be sliced into feathery stars that form a constellation in a clear broth.

A slaw, made from finely chopped red cabbage and lemony mayonnaise, is a cool foil for piping hot, sautéed winged beans spiked with garlic.

Winged Beans with Red Cabbage

❖ ❖ ❖

1 head red cabbage

1 cup lemony mayonnaise
(see recipe, page 269)

1 pound winged beans

3 tablespoons butter

½ cup chopped fresh parsley

2 cloves garlic, peeled and minced

Salt and pepper

Quarter and core the cabbage, then shred the quarters in a food processor. Transfer to a salad bowl and toss well with the mayonnaise. Refrigerate until ready to serve. ❖ *Steam the winged beans for 4 minutes, or until tender. Cool, then thinly slice.* ❖ *In a saucepan, melt the butter. Add the parsley, garlic, and salt and pepper to taste. Cook over medium heat, stirring with a wooden spoon. Add the sliced winged beans and sauté for several minutes. Transfer to a serving dish.* ❖ *Serve with the red cabbage on the side.* ❖ Yield: 6 servings

FAVA BEAN

My mother and I are so alike and yet so different. I shall use fava beans as an illustration of this state of affairs. We both love ful medames—*dried fava beans cooked until tender and mashed with olive oil, lemon, and garlic. Colette and I often get into our Arab mode on Sundays, scooping up the flavorful beans with pita bread at noon. Then I am her Egyptian attendant for the afternoon—washing her hair, filing and polishing her nails, massaging her calves—while she tells me stories of her youth spent in Cairo.*

When it comes to the fresh fava bean, we part ways. First, we differ on its name. Colette calls it a broad bean. How infuriating! "How can you possibly call that tender, springtime, light green bud nestled with its brothers in a large and noble pod that dull and awkward name?" I yell. "Well," she counters with an energetic huff, "fava, or fève, *isn't English. Here, they're called broad beans and this is where I live! And they are broad!"*

Colette is enthusiastic when fava beans appear in her favorite produce market. I turn up my nose. Why? Because I like to eat them raw, the way I did in France, with sweet butter, bread, and coarse salt. We would pile them high, unshelled, right on a wooden table for each person to open. The Mâcon, dry and clear, flowed endlessly.

But Colette is uninterested in raw broad beans; in the United States fava beans are harvested too old to eat raw. She sautés them gently with olive oil, shiitake mushrooms, and a sprinkling of fresh sage, with a touch of lemon juice, a pat of butter, and freshly ground pepper. I suppose I have to admit that I eat more broad beans than anyone when it is

◄ Young fava beans, seen here both whole and shelled, can be eaten raw as an hors d'oeuvre, with salt, pepper, olive oil, and slices of crusty country bread.

Colette who cooks them. But I still miss those long spring evenings and my "fèves crues."

We do agree, however, on fried, salted Chinese broad beans. These brown, crisp, tasty beans are the best snack in the world. They are available in many Oriental grocery stores.

AVAILABILITY:
April to July.

SHOPPING GUIDE:
Select full, light green pods. Avoid those with excessive discoloration or yellowing. Open a pod and taste a bean; it should not be bitter.

STORAGE:
Will keep for 2 to 3 days, wrapped in plastic, in the vegetable drawer of the refrigerator.

A field of fava beans, onions, and salad greens in New Jersey, where small farms still exist amid giant industrial parks.

Fava Beans with Golden Mushrooms

• • •

4 pounds fava beans in the pod

2 tablespoons butter

I pound golden chanterelles or other wild mushrooms, quickly rinsed and drained

Salt and pepper

I tablespoon chopped fresh chives

Shell the beans and steam for 5 minutes, or until barely tender. Set aside. ❖ *In a skillet, melt the butter. Add the mushrooms and sauté for several minutes over medium heat. Add the beans and cook for another 2 to 3 minutes. Season with salt, pepper and the chives to taste.*
❖ Yield: 4 servings

....

A simple yet sublimely elegant dish, sautéed fava beans are combined with chanterelles and seasoned with salt, pepper, and chives.

BULBS

When I first came to the United States, I felt homesick whenever I saw leeks in supermarkets. The aroma of leek-and-potato soup slowly cooking in the concierge's apartment is what makes an apartment building truly French. The leeks, cut in half-inch pieces, simmering with diced potatoes in a good vegetable broth, smell divine. I always wanted to eat dinner with the concierge. I would imagine myself sitting in her dining room, dunking a piece of crusty French bread in the hot soup. I could never quite reproduce this marvelous soup in New York, because years ago store-bought leeks were tough; besides, my husband disliked potatoes in soup. But he liked large slices of raw onion on his hamburgers, and I hated that; they were too strong. Everything changed when I met Peggy Kenney, who was then managing a five-acre farm for the Rare Fruit Council International in Miami, Florida. Peggy traveled the world, collecting seeds and plant materials she thought could grow in Florida. Through her I met Charles Smolen, a first-generation farmer. She told me that Charles was performing miracles with vegetables and growing new species.

Charles's farm was at the end of a long dirt road. It had been difficult to get him to see me. He was very suspicious of journalists, for he felt that his secrets would be stolen. He started his plantation with five acres, and today he has 160 acres. With the help of Vicky Drane, his partner, and a group of Mexican workers, he grows extraordinary things—magnificent chilies and herbs, lilliputian lemon-drop squash, tiny zucchini (green and yellow), mâche, purple *haricots verts*, and watercress with no water. His African rosemary was so pungent that you could smell it miles away. What enchanted me most was his tiny spring onions, so tender and mild that you could munch on them right

Fennel

Asparagus

Garlic

Scallon, onion, leek, and ramp

◄ A country bowl of pearl onions. Each variety has a slightly different flavor; all are worth the time it takes to peel them.

there and then, and his perfect miniature leeks and fennel. I left with a full bag, and back home I served the best *soupe aux poireaux et pommes de terre* that I had ever made! I even served, with pleasure, hamburgers with Charles's spring onions.

A few days later, I flew to San Diego, California, to meet Tom Chino, who, with his parents and sister, runs the Chino Farm. Tom's parents came from Japan just after the war and settled outside of Bosque del Ranch, a few miles out of San Diego. They started with five acres and grew treasured Japanese vegetables. Today, the farm covers forty acres and is run by Tom. Chino farm does not ship its produce but sells the day's pickings from a stand. People drive hundreds of miles to buy these superb vegetables and carefully grown salad greens. As Tom and I walked through the field, he picked up what I thought was an overgrown spring onion. "This," he said, "is a Japanese leek." The tall, narrow, white leek, with a few inches of green leaves, was right away thrust into my hands. Then others followed, and a few minutes later I had a bouquet of strong sweet-smelling leeks—enough for a whole meal for my family. I continued walking with Tom, past a field of long white and red radishes, strange-looking greens, and turnips no bigger than my pinky. I suddenly wished that I could live in San Diego. Oh, the wonderful dishes I would prepare! I left San Diego loaded with boxes of vegetables, thinking about how I would surprise Marianne.

Onions can be as small as a marble or as large as a softball, and can be eaten raw, fried, baked, braised. . . . The possibilities are endless. Pictured here are pearl onions, red onions, yellow onions, Spanish onions, and white onions. ▶

FENNEL

"You're like me," my mother tells me every so often. "You have a Mediterranean disposition." I've inherited her hot-blooded spirit, it seems, and also her love of fennel. This tangy, licorice-flavored substitute for celery gives us both a taste of the sun even in the dead of winter, and we like that. But it wasn't Colette who first introduced me to fennel. I shall set the scene. Port-la-Galère, a resort town on the Riviera, between Nice and Cannes. I was fifteen—such an impressionable age— and madly in love with Jean-Marc, who was spending the summer there, too. We were at a party that my aunt gave for all the young people once a year. It was a warm night and he led me out onto the balcony. He spoke of his plans for the following year and about how difficult our classes would be. When he put his arm around me, I knew a kiss (my first) would follow. I also remembered that I had eaten a piece of bread slathered with aioli. Excusing myself with a timid smile, I ran off to find my aunt in the kitchen. I explained my predicament. She laughed heartily, cut open a bulb of fennel and handed me a large piece. "Eat," she said, "quickly." So I chewed on the crunchy, sweet-tasting chunk and felt my mouth refreshed. I ran back to the balcony to receive my first, much-anticipated kiss, but Jean-Marc had disappeared. I spied him later that evening dancing with Martine and my heart broke—for about three days. Then I fell in love with Grégoire and bit into fresh fennel before our first date!

About the size of a man's fist, a fennel bulb is made up of celery-like stalks topped with feathery leaves. Both the leaves and bulb may be used in cooking. Fennel is delicious raw, dipped in olive oil and salt, and in all manner of salads. It adds zest to stews and may be braised in the same manner as Belgian endive. Fennel soup is aromatic and healthful.

AVAILABILITY:
July to March.

SHOPPING GUIDE:
Select unbruised bulbs with tightly wrapped stalks. Avoid bulbs that have been trimmed excessively.

STORAGE:
Will keep for 5 to 6 days, wrapped in plastic, in the vegetable drawer of the refrigerator.

We like to munch on sweet, licorice-flavored bulbs of fennel as we cook dinner; its sun-drenched crunch whets the appetite.

Fennel with Spiced Coarse Salt

◆ ◆ ◆

This is a very simple appetizer that our Chinese friend Cindy Wo taught us. She served it with sliced daikon. We liked it so much that we tried substituting several other raw vegetables for the daikon. Fennel won out!

3 fennel bulbs, trimmed

1/2 cup coarse salt

1/4 teaspoon hot sesame oil*

Freshly ground black pepper

1 tablespoon black sesame seeds

Quarter the fennel bulbs and thinly slice them lengthwise. Place in a bowl of ice water until ready to serve. ❖ *In a bowl, mix the salt with the sesame oil and pepper to taste. Heat a cast-iron skillet. When the skillet is hot, add the salt and cook over high heat, stirring constantly, for about 3 minutes, or until the salt is dry. Remove from the heat and cool. Add the black sesame seeds and mix well. (This spiced salt will keep several weeks in a tightly sealed container.)* ❖ *Drain the fennel slices and arrange them in a circle on a round serving platter. Place a small bowl of spiced salt in the center.*

*Hot sesame oil is flavored with hot chilies.

Sliced fennel with a spicy dipping salt, Italian breadsticks, and a carafe of extra-virgin olive oil. Slivered red pickled ginger garnishes this simple summer hors d'oeuvre.

Braised Fennel with Mussels

• • •

2 fennel bulbs, trimmed

4 tablespoons butter

1 tablespoon olive oil

1 tablespoon sugar

¾ cup chicken broth

Salt and pepper

3 cloves garlic, peeled and chopped

2 cups minced fresh parsley

½ cup white wine

2 pounds mussels, scrubbed

Quarter the fennel bulbs. In a large saucepan, melt 2 tablespoons of the butter with the oil. When the butter is hot, add the fennel and sauté for 5 minutes on each side. Sprinkle the fennel with the sugar and cook for another 3 minutes. Add the broth, lower the heat, cover, and simmer for 15 minutes. Season with salt and pepper to taste. Remove from the heat and set aside. ❖ *In a large heavy-bottomed saucepan, melt the remaining butter. When the butter is hot, add the garlic and sauté for 2 to 3 minutes. Add the parsley and white wine. Stir once and cook for 1 minute. Add the mussels, shake the saucepan, cover, and lower the heat to medium. Cook for 5 minutes, or until the mussels open. Remove from the heat.* ❖ *Place the mussels on a large serving platter with their liquid. Surround with the braised fennel and serve.*

❖ Yield: 4 servings

. . . .

Mussels are made to be matched with garlic and parsley, as in *moules marinieres*. The sweetness of braised fennel is an ideal addition to this classic dish. A crusty baguette will be used to soak up the fragrant sauce.

ASPARAGUS

I have always been a staunch supporter of good table manners; I have even begun to reprimand my son, who, at the tender age of one, lets me know he has finished his meal by tossing the last bits nonchalantly over the side of the table. Later on, I will remind him to close his mouth when chewing, to remove his elbows from the table, and to cut his meat with the knife in his right hand. There is one rule, however, that I bend for myself and will bend for him: thou shalt not eat with thine hands. When it comes to asparagus, using a fork is a sin. Brushed with melted butter, asparagus was made to be eaten tender tip to mouth, nibbled down to just before the "wood," the stem end held delicately between thumb and forefinger. Why do I bestow this honor on the asparagus? I simply can't imagine cutting into or piercing such a perfectly formed natural object with such a divine yet earthy taste.

From its treatment at the table, we will reverse our steps and discuss its preparation at the kitchen counter. First question: how much to trim off the ends? I am admittedly ruthless here, preferring to whack off a large portion of the fibrous bottom in order to spare the eater the embarrassment of leaving stringy stubs on the plate. Question number two: to scrape or to peel? At this step, I relent a little, and find myself gently scraping just the finest layer from the stem end. Finally, to steam or to boil? Maman, you're going to kill me but...I like to boil. The stalks must be tied with kitchen string and immersed, stem ends down, in lots and lots of salted water. I've always found steaming such a hefty vegetable as the asparagus a bit mean-spirited; furthermore, the stalks seem to toughen if not immersed.

Years ago, there was just one type of asparagus available at neighborhood greengrocers. Plump and green, quite unrefined, the perennial common aspara-gus has a pronounced, earthy flavor and is especially good in purees and soups. Now, a popular "pencil" asparagus has swept stalk-lovers off their feet. Although milder in taste, the elegant, bright green, skinny stalks are a pleasure to bite into and, blanched, make a wonderful addition to spring salads. Of course, nothing can compare to Argenteuil asparagus and white Belgian asparagus. Fat, tender, unabashedly perfumed like wild mushrooms or upturned meadowland soil, these prize stalks are difficult to come by fresh in the United States. Pity. But they are so good that, even in jars, their superior quality shines through. It is not surprising that the Sun King, Louis XIV, was fond of them.

I share Marianne's enchantment with the glorious Parisian spring, when white Argenteuil asparagus first appears in the outdoor markets. Its mellow and buttery taste requires a simple sprinkle of vinaigrette or a dab of light, lemony mayonnaise. My enchanted daughter, however, failed to include the fact that white asparagus is grown in the United States as well.

The first pale stalks to appear in our markets a few years ago came from Chile. We all rushed to buy them, only to be disappointed by their woody texture and bland flavor. At about the same time, several young farmers from California's Sonoma Valley decided to try growing white asparagus. The problem was the expense of blanching: to prevent asparagus from turning green, the crop must be covered with earth. Most farmers found this method too expensive and abandoned the idea. My longing for white asparagus seemed to be doomed until last spring, when I visited the Sonoma Valley and met Greg Nilsen of Wine and Country Cuisine. Greg distributes produce grown by his friends all over the Sonoma Valley. When I talked to Greg about my longing for white asparagus, he told me I was in for a surprise. We drove to a suburban development outside Santa Rosa and stopped in front of a two-story house. There, I was greeted by Ed Doyle, who led me to his backyard. I looked in astonishment at the even rows of thick cardboard boxes, standing upside-down like soldiers at attention. "What asparagus!" said Ed in a proud voice. "I buy the boxes at the post office. Covering the stalks with cardboard is cheaper and works just as well." I lifted a box and—lo and behold—underneath were the whitest asparagus I had ever seen. That night, we gobbled up white asparagus with melted butter and lemon. They were excellent, but not quite as superb as the French ones. Ed assured me that next year's crop would be even better. The post office will be pleased... but not as pleased as I!

AVAILABILITY:
March to June.

SHOPPING GUIDE:
Select plump, crisp-looking asparagus with tightly furled tips. Avoid those with shriveled skin and spreading tips.

STORAGE:
Will keep for 1 to 2 days, loosely wrapped in plastic, in the vegetable drawer of the refrigerator.

White Asparagus with Passion Fruit Vinaigrette

• • •

2 pounds white asparagus

1 cup fresh red currants

½ tablespoon red-wine vinegar

2 tablespoons olive oil

Salt and pepper

2 passion fruits

With a vegetable peeler, peel the bottom 4 inches of each asparagus stem. Then cut about 1 inch off the bottom with a sharp knife. Steam the asparagus until tender. Transfer to a serving platter and sprinkle with the red currants. ❖ *In a bowl, combine the vinegar, oil, and salt and pepper to taste.* ❖ *Cut the passion fruits in half across. Using a demitasse spoon, remove the juice and seeds and place in a small bowl. Strain the juice through a fine sieve, pushing the pulp through with the back of a wooden spoon to get all the juice. Add the juice to the vinaigrette and adjust the seasoning.* ❖ *Serve the asparagus with the vinaigrette on the side.* ❖ *Yield: 4 servings*

▲
Bold in flavor as well as in design, this dish of exotic white asparagus is sauced with a fruit-based vinaigrette.

Sold from a private doorstep, broccoli, asparagus, yellow corn, and Swiss chard come directly from a backyard garden is San Miguel, Mexico. ▶

GARLIC

As long as I can remember, I have loved garlic. My after-school *gouter* (snack) consisted of a piece of baguette doused in olive oil and rubbed with garlic. My brother, traditional as he was, would request chocolate with his bread. Once we had eaten, I would chase after him, blowing him garlic kisses. How he despised both me and my garlic breath! When he ran to my mother screaming for help, she would calm him down by saying, "Wait till she has a boyfriend... she'll stop then."

I fell in love at the age of eight with Henri. I stopped eating garlic. I didn't know then that garlic was an aphrodisiac. I learned about those powers only many years later, on my honeymoon. My husband and I were traveling through Sicily and stopped one night at a small inn outside of Agrigento, a town famous for its intact Greek temple. The innkeeper's wife cooed generously at our newlywed bliss and left a garland of garlic under my pillow. When questioned the next morning, she explained, "The garlic will make him love you forever!" I have been married now nearly thirty years, and I'm sure she was right!

Besides its powers in the realm of love, garlic has been (and still is) considered to have medicinal and salutary value. The frescoes inside the Great Pyramid at Giza depict slaves eating garlic and onions for strength. During the fifteenth century, garlic was believed to cure consumption, toothaches, and snake bites. My own grandmother used garlic on sties and my best friend, the painter Arakawa, thinks that garlic should be an important part of the daily diet, that it wards off sickness and supplies pure energy to the system.

Ever since my honeymoon, I've used tons of garlic in my cooking, as an aromatic. Recently, however, I learned to use garlic not as a flavoring agent, but on its own, as a vegetable. I was in Corsica when

I first tasted garlic soup and whole heads of garlic baked in white wine. The soft flesh from the cloves was spread on country bread with the local goat cheese.

More recently still, I visited Gilroy, California, the so-called Garlic Capital of the United States. Every year, sometimes every two years, the town of Gilroy, which is surrounded by farms growing enormous quantities of garlic, has a festival. The festival is a collective effort on the part of the town's officials, growers, and inhabitants, who pride themselves on having invented the most recipes using garlic. There is a Garlic Queen, parades, music, and, above all, food. Stands with garlic garlands, dolls made with garlic, appetizers, relishes, interesting dishes, etc. Everyone has a great time.

I sampled green garlic ravioli tossed with melted butter and grated parmesan; a veal fricassee cooked with hundreds (literally!) of garlic cloves; elephant garlic stuffed with minced pork; and garlic popcorn balls. I was disappointed, all the same, not to find a recipe for a garlic dessert (I'm still working on it)! Now,

garlic from the braids hanging in my kitchen often ends up roasted as a side dish for beef or pork or caramelized as an appetizer. Marianne scolds me often, claiming that I overdo the garlic. But she makes garlic bread with so many cloves it makes me reel. Such a typical daughter!

AVAILABILITY:
All year round; best in spring.

SHOPPING GUIDE:
Select medium heads, with heavy, full, firm cloves. Very large cloves and elephant garlic are slightly bitter but milder in taste.

STORAGE:
Will keep for several weeks, in a basket, in a dry, airy place.

▲

Bulbs of regular and elephant garlic. Both can be baked whole and eaten as a fragrant spread on crusty loaves.

Baked Stuffed Elephant Garlic

◆ ◆ ◆

Recently, we came across a ready-made cream cheese mixed with pesto sauce that is excellent to use as a stuffing. If this cream cheese is not available in your market, you can prepare it yourself in no time: simply combine thoroughly one part pesto to three parts cream cheese and refrigerate until ready to use. Serve the stuffed garlic as a main dish for lunch along with a green salad, country bread, and a bottle of chilled white wine.

16 cloves elephant garlic, peeled

$\frac{1}{2}$ pound pesto cream cheese

2 tablespoons olive oil

Salt and pepper

Parsley sprigs for garnish

Preheat the oven to 375 degrees.
❖   *Cut a very thin slice from the convex side of each clove so that it can sit on a plate. With a small melon baller cut an oblong trough in the concave side of each clove. Fill with the cream cheese mixture.* ❖   *Place the garlic cloves in a baking pan. Drizzle with olive oil, sprinkle with salt and pepper, and bake for 20 minutes, or until golden brown.* ❖   *Arrange 4 stuffed cloves on each of 4 salad plates, garnish with parsley, and serve.* ❖   *Yield: 4 servings*

....

Elephant garlic stuffed with a mixture of pesto and cream cheese and baked. The cheese is made of layers of fresh cream cheese and pesto.

When serving a basket of crudités was the latest rage, my impulse was to grab and bite into a crisp scallion, an impulse I would regret for the remainder of the evening as I watched other guests drift away from me. In my mind, I would transport myself to a Greek isle, where I could munch on scallions, fresh bread, and olives without a care. I've tried to mask the scent by sucking on mints, chewing gum, and eating parsley, all to no avail. Nowadays, I cook scallions, a process that removes their odor. Happily, cooked scallions can be an elegant and unusual appetizer or vegetable when served with a piquant sauce.

In Egypt, where I grew up, onions were part of our everyday diet. The national dish, *ful medames,* made with brown fava beans, is always served with chopped spring onions. My father used to tell me that each pharaoh distributed bunches of onions to his workers so that they would build him a better pyramid than his predecessor's. My mother was more practical: "When an onion has three thick layers of skin, winter will be cold," she predicted. From onion lore to a braid of red onions hanging in my kitchen, I've made the fragrant globe part of my life. A real French onion soup bubbling with melted gruyère and golden brown croutons is heaven on earth. And Marianne makes the best onion jam. She hasn't let me have her recipe, since she likes to give it to her father on his birthday in an old Mason jar with a navy blue ribbon and a flower.

I can't carry a tune—or so everyone tells me. One day, I read that the Emperor Nero ate leeks every day to improve his voice. I immediately went on a leek diet but, to my chagrin, my voice didn't take on dulcet tones. However, I eat leeks with great pleasure and become homesick as soon as I breathe in their aroma. My friend Mireille swears by them. She once told me that, if

◄ The "skinny" onions. From right to left: Japanese leeks, leeks, ramps, and scallions.

Lily-white and dark green spring onions at a market in San Miguel de Allende, in central Mexico.

I wanted to lose five pounds fast, I should live on steamed leeks for three days. I've never tried it but one day I will. Leeks also helped me to win over my mother-in-law, who was Welsh. It seems that the Welsh overcame the Saxons in the sixth century by wearing leeks in their caps to distinguish themselves from the Saxons in a ferocious battle. Leeks are superb steamed whole with a lemony vinaigrette, or added to eggs for a scrumptious quiche, in soup, or stuffed in fish. My favorite way of using leeks is to cut them in fine julienne and deep-fry them for one minute. A mound of fried leeks along with a broiled steak, a salad, and cherries is one of the best meals I can think of.

I had never heard of ramps—wild leeks—until I went on a trip through Georgia a few years ago. We were walking along a river bank when my host, a local farmer, Georges Fresh, led me into the woods. There, he pointed out hundreds of broad, dark-green leaves called ramps. "The leaves and bulbs are delicious," said my friend, "but their smell could kill a hog!" We picked some nonetheless and steamed them for dinner. He was right about their pungent odor: it lingered in the kitchen—and on my hands—for days. I liked their slightly bitter taste but thought I could do without the odor. So I brought some home to Marianne, who fell in love with them. She began to develop recipes even with her husband ranting and bringing up the fans from the basement. He gave in when he tasted her ramps with baby golden beets and salmon caviar. The ramps were tied together in bunches; the dish not only tasted wonderful but looked superb! I still won't prepare ramps in my house, though. I just go to Marianne's.

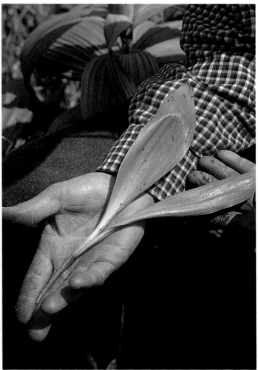

A young, tender ramp, just picked.

Wild ramps in the field. Ramps have an intriguing, powerful flavor, a mix of leek and scallion.

Pearl Onion   This is a tiny (about the size of a marble), globe-shaped onion with white, red, or yellow skin, often sold in pint baskets. They take a long time to peel, but they are worth the trouble. They can be pickled, braised, boiled, or deep-fried, and they are a lovely addition to mixed spring vegetables.

Yellow Onion   This medium-sized onion is the most commonly used for cooking. Yellow onions are firm and strongly flavored. The globe-shaped ones are the best for cooking. Large Vidalia onions, grown in Georgia and available only in spring and early summer, are very sweet and moist, excellent tossed in salads, served atop hamburgers, or chopped in stuffing.

Spanish Onion   This is a very large yellow onion, mild and sweet, that is excellent to serve raw in salad or with cold meats. Try sautéing or deep-frying Spanish onions.

White Onion   The large variety of this onion is referred to as the Bermuda onion. Like the Spanish onion, it is good deep-fried but can be eaten raw, chopped, or stewed into onion jam.

Red Onion   The red onion is mild in taste and varied in size. Large ones are best for eating raw in salads or with broiled meats. They are sometimes available braided in a rope, to be hung in a cool place in the kitchen.

General rules for all onions:

- Scallions, onions, and leeks should be cut with a very sharp knife.
- If you are sensitive to onion fumes, peel and cut them next to running water. It will help.
- Leftover onions should be kept no longer than 24 hours, tightly wrapped.
- Avoid using the food processor to chop onions as the blade tends to bruise the onions. Use only with a slicing blade for onion soup or fried onions.

AVAILABILITY:
Scallions and onions: all year round. Leeks: all year round; peak season October to March. Ramps: spring.

STORAGE:
Scallions will keep for over 1 week, in a sealed plastic bag, in the vegetable drawer of the refrigerator. Onions will keep for up to 1 month in a basket in a cool, airy place. Leeks and ramps will keep for 3-4 days, wrapped in plastic, in the vegetable drawer of the refrigerator.

SHOPPING GUIDE:
Select crisp and fresh-looking scallions with a bright white bulb, dark green leaves, and firm texture; avoid those that have been trimmed excessively. Select spotless onions with thin skins and hard tops; avoid those that are sprouting. Select small to medium fresh-looking leeks with the white parts and roots intact. Select ramps with bright green leaves and firm white heads.

Scallions growing in a field in Santa Rosa, California, amid the pretty flowers of mustard plants. ▶

Steamed Scallions with Black Olives

⬩ ⬩ ⬩

This is the type of appetizer that can be easily prepared in advance, or even at the last minute. The garnish and the fresh herbs will give it a special touch.

20 scallions, trimmed (3 bunches)

¼ pound black Greek olives, pitted

Rosebuds for garnish (optional)

1 tablespoon chopped fresh thyme

1 cup zucchini-wasabi sauce (see recipe, page 271)

Steam or poach the scallions for 2 minutes. Using a spatula, transfer them to a platter. ❖ To serve, fan 5 scallions on each of 4 individual serving plates. Garnish with black olives and rosebuds (if desired), and sprinkle with fresh thyme. Serve the zucchini-wasabi sauce on the side.

❖ Yield: 4 servings

....

▼ The modest bulb dressed in finery: a fan of steamed scallions, garnished with black olives, edible rosebuds, and wood ear mushrooms.

Onions need not be relegated to the role of seasoning other food. Here, whole onions are cooked and filled with roasted red peppers, seasoned with vinaigrette, and accented with pomegranate in a visually striking salad.

Onion Salad with Pomegranates

◆ ◆ ◆

12 small white or yellow onions, peeled

1 4-ounce jar sweet red peppers

Salt and pepper

1 tablespoon red-wine vinegar

2 tablespoons vegetable oil

2 pomegranates

Place the onions in a saucepan and cover with boiling water. Lower the heat and simmer for 15 minutes, or until the onions are tender but not overcooked. Drain and refresh under cold water. Drain again. ❖ With the point of a sharp knife, make a hole in the center of each onion. ❖ Drain the peppers, reserving the liquid. Cut the peppers into small pieces and stuff the onions with them. Pour the pepper liquid over the onions with oil, vinegar, and salt and pepper to taste. Toss well. ❖ Cut the pomegranates in half and separate the seeds from the membranes. ❖ Line a salad bowl with the pomegranate seeds, arrange the onions on top, and serve. ❖ Yield: 4 servings

Honey-sweet Vidalia onions compete with peaches in our warm state of Georgia. Here, a Vidalia onion is baked until tender and sauced with mango puree.

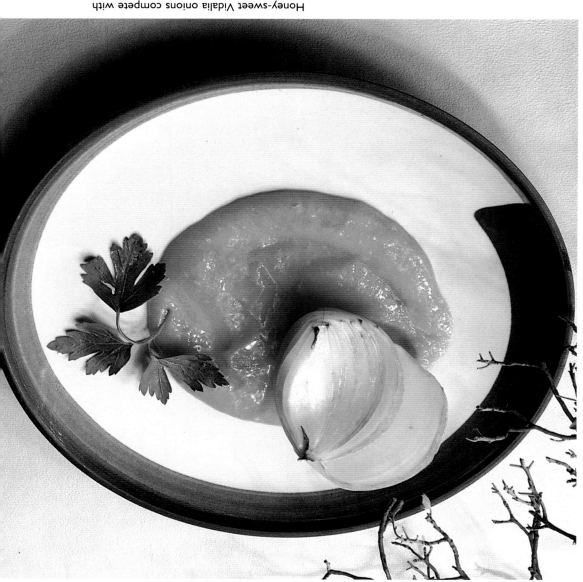

Baked Onion with Mango Puree

◆ ◆ ◆

For this recipe, use Bermuda or Vidalia onions.

2 large white sweet onions, peeled

1 tablespoon olive oil

1 tablespoon soy sauce

³/₄ cup chicken broth

2 ripe mangoes

Freshly ground black pepper

2 sprigs fresh mint, leaves only

Preheat the oven to 350 degrees. ❖ Cut each onion in half across. Arrange the onion halves, flat side down, on an oiled baking dish. Combine the olive oil and soy sauce and brush over the onions. Add the chicken broth and bake until the tops are golden brown, about 20 minutes. ❖ Peel the mangoes. Cut the flesh into chunks and puree in a food processor. ❖ Place some mango puree on each of 4 individual serving plates. Arrange the onion halves on top, carefully spreading the onion layers apart. Season with freshly ground pepper to taste and garnish with fresh mint leaves. ❖ Yield: 4 servings

Crispy fried strips of leek share a platter with sautéed wood ear mushrooms to create a dish of contrasts. Radish sprouts are tossed on top for an informal garnish.

Fried Leeks with Wood Ear Mushrooms

♦ ♦ ♦

Wood ear mushrooms can be found fresh in California and in Oriental grocery stores.

This dish is a play of contrasts. The combination of crisp strips of fried leeks, with their mildly oniony flavor, and the soft mushrooms, with their earthy taste, makes this a wonderful dish for a summer dinner alfresco.

2 fresh wood ear mushrooms or 3 ounces
dried wood ear mushrooms, soaked for
15 minutes in warm water

6 leeks

Oil for frying

2 tablespoons olive oil

Salt and pepper

Japanese watercress or
radish sprouts for garnish

Cut the wood ear mushrooms into bite-size pieces and set aside. ❖ *Trim and wash the leeks. Cut off about 3 inches from the green part; cut each leek in half lengthwise. Cut each half lengthwise into thin strips.* ❖ *Fill a deep-fryer to its capacity with oil and heat to 360 degrees. Fry a handful of leeks at a time until golden brown. Using a slotted spatula, transfer the strips to paper towels. Continue frying until all the leeks are cooked. Keep them warm and crisp in a very low oven until ready to serve.* ❖ *In a skillet, heat the olive oil. Add the mushrooms and sauté for 2 to 3 minutes. Season with salt and pepper to taste.* ❖ *Place the fried leeks on a platter along with the wood ear mushrooms. Garnish with Japanese watercress and serve.* ❖ *Yield: 4 servings*

Ramps with Miniature Golden Beets

❖ ❖ ❖

2 pounds miniature golden beets

16 ramps

8 scallions, green part only

$\frac{1}{2}$ cup lemon vinaigrette
(see recipe, page 269)

3 ounces fresh salmon caviar

2 lemons, thinly sliced

Trim the beets, leaving about 2 inches of stem. In a saucepan, bring 1 quart of water to a boil. Add the beets, lower the heat to medium, and cook until tender, about 15 minutes. Drain and peel. Set aside. ❖ *Clean and trim the ramps. Place the ramps side by side in a large skillet. Cover with boiling water and simmer for 5 minutes. Drain on paper towels.* ❖ *Soften the scallions in hot water and cut into long, thin strips. Tie 4 ramps together using scallion "string." Arrange the ramps on 4 individual serving plates along with the beets. Pour some lemon vinaigrette over the ramps and beets. Garnish with salmon caviar and lemon slices.*
❖ Yield: 4 servings

. . . .

A bunch of steamed ramps, tied with string and bejeweled with fresh salmon caviar, is served with miniature golden beets. A lemon vinaigrette seasons this stunning, warm salad.

MINIATURE
VEGETABLES

In the late seventies, when the French chef Paul Bocuse and his friends began transforming classic French cuisine into nouvelle cuisine, I was most fascinated by their influence on vegetables. Picked very young or trimmed to be small and uniform, vegetables were arranged on the plate in vivid patterns, forming a star or a fan of butter-varnished color. Even their texture and taste were changed. Instead of preparing soft, stewed, creamy mixtures, these innovative chefs steamed each vegetable until it was not quite tender, resistant to the tooth, so that its true nature, fresh and untouched, could be relished.

America was more than ready for nouvelle cuisine. Almost as soon as American chefs adopted this new French method of cooking, it was again transformed to accommodate American palates and culinary culture. California's younger farmers soon took on the challenge of creating vegetables worthy of such a refined cuisine. Genes were twisted, directed, diverted until the desired result was at hand: tiny, perfect, tasty versions of countless vegetables. Pinky-sized carrots, zucchini, and corn; beets no larger than a walnut; fennel bulbs that fit in the palm of a hand; pencil-thin leeks; pattypan squash the size of a quarter...it seemed that no vegetable was spared.

I, too, succumbed to the appeal of miniature vegetables, especially after visiting the Chino farm outside of San Diego, California. I arrived early one morning at the farm and was greeted by Tom Chino's oldest son, a handsome Japanese-American. He began my tour with the zucchini bed; he pulled one out, washed it with water poured from a bottle, and handed it to me. The tiny zucchini was crisp, tender, and fragrant. White turnips were next (why did he insist on giving me only one? I wanted more!), followed by miniature spring

◄ Soaking up the sun in a country garden, miniature vegetables are jewels to be treated with a delicate hand. From right: turnips, beets, white eggplants, and carrots.

onions and tomatoes so small they looked like tiny grapes. And as we walked back to my car, he handed me a jar of pickled eggplants, the smallest I had ever seen. Convinced that the future of vegetables lay in the world of lilliputians, I came back to New York resolved never to use any vegetable bigger than my pinky! Marianne convinced me, after a few battles, that there is nothing wrong with eating regular-size squash or fat leeks or hefty eggplants, as long as they are in season. Actually, she only half-convinced me.

My mother is clearly fascinated by the esthetic aspect of vegetables. Not to say that I am uninterested; I would never place a tomato on the same plate with a carrot, nor would I allow the murky, brown flesh of an eggplant to leave my kitchen counter unadorned. But these natural reactions to color co-ordination are mild compared to my mother's application of her esthetic rules. It is primarily for esthetic reasons, then, that she was thrilled when miniature vegetables became available in her favorite gourmet produce store. She marveled at their size: she wouldn't have to peel or slice or trim anything in order to have jewels bedeck her plate. And because they all took about the same time to cook, she could play with color and shape as much as she wished without repeating herself.

But at first, I grumbled at her frequent forays into the microcosmos. The vegetables she brought home were unnatural, said I, just fad food like gourmet popcorn, chocolate-dipped frozen bananas, the kiwi. We already had good corn—why did it have to shrink to the size of a cornichon? Why did summer squashes have to be made unstuffable, beets unsliceable, and carrots too tiny to hold?

I found out why. Requiring a minimum of cooking to bring out their superior flavor, the minis are sweeter, tenderer, infinitely more delectable than their fatter, bigger, tougher relatives. I am now a loyal fan and will occasion-

ally dig deep into my pocket for that extra dollar in order to have a meal of beautiful miniature vegetables. But only occasionally. After all, my mother is small and I am tall, and every size should get a fair chance at being a star.

AVAILABILITY:
All year round for most; spring and summer for corn and fennel.

SHOPPING GUIDE:
Select firm, unblemished vegetables.

STORAGE:
Will keep for 2 to 3 days, wrapped in plastic, in the vegetable drawer of the refrigerator. Best eaten the same day they are bought.

A Sonoma Valley farmer digging up his favorite crop: pencil-thin miniature leeks.

"Scaled" down and ready to be steamed "au naturel," an assortment of miniature squash, eggplant, and cauliflower.

Steamed Miniature Vegetables with Carrot Sauce

◆ ◆ ◆

This simple dish calls for more than three miniature vegetables. Use different shapes and colors so that the dish looks appetizing.

2 pounds miniature vegetables, such as
carrots, turnips, zucchini,
zucchini flowers, beets, etc.

Salt and pepper

2 cups carrot sauce
(see recipe, page 268)

Trim the vegetables. Leave about 1 inch of stem on the carrots, turnips, and beets. Cook zucchini flowers separately, as they are very fragile. ❖ *Steam the vegetables according to hardness; beets first, then carrots, then zucchini, squash, corn, etc., together.* ❖ *Arrange on a serving platter and sprinkle with salt and pepper to taste. Serve the carrot sauce separately.* ❖ Yield: 4 servings

....

Barely steamed, tender miniature vegetables are served with a seasoned carrot sauce.

Tom Thumb tomatoes are even smaller—and sweeter—than cherry tomatoes.

Sonoma Valley, at the forefront of miniaturization, produces tiny romaine lettuces and watercress.

A new hybrid of cherry tomatoes with a bright yellow hue.

A panoply of raw miniature vegetables surrounding a "zabaglione" made with veal stock and frothy egg yolks instead of the traditional Marsala.

Miniature Vegetable Crudités with Savory Zabaglione

• • •

We recommend serving cool miniature vegetables on a hot summer day when cooking is *verboten*. The zabaglione sauce, made with a concentrated veal stock instead of the traditional marsala wine, is a welcome change from vinaigrette or any of the so-called dips. Miniature beets and leeks should be cooked; all other vegetables can be eaten raw.

2 pounds miniature vegetables, such as zucchini, squash, carrots, or fennel

Coarse salt

Freshly ground pepper

4 egg yolks

Grated zest of ½ lemon

1 ½ cups veal stock*

Salt and white pepper

*Available commercially in frozen form.

Divide the vegetables among 4 individual serving plates. Lightly sprinkle with coarse salt and freshly ground pepper to taste. ❖ *Place the egg yolks in a bowl with the lemon zest. Beat with an electric beater until the mixture is thick and pale yellow. Then place the bowl in the top part of a double boiler over simmering water and continue to beat, adding the veal stock very gradually. When the sauce is thick and frothy, season with salt and white pepper to taste. Pour the savory zabaglione into a sauceboat. Serve alongside the vegetables.* ❖ Yield: 4 servings

Fennel no bigger than a thumb are adorned with miniature tomato "pearls."

Miniature Fennel with Tomatoes

• • •

This dish should be served at room temperature as an appetizer along with ice-cold beer or iced aquavit.

4 miniature fennel bulbs,
trimmed and
split in half

3 tablespoons butter

2 ripe tomatoes

Salt and pepper

1 6-ounce jar pickled pearl onions

Parsley sprigs for garnish

In a saucepan, bring 1 quart of salted water to a boil. Add the fennel and cook over medium heat for 5 minutes. Drain. ❖ *In a skillet, melt the butter and add the fennel halves. Sauté for several minutes, or until lightly browned. Set aside to cool.* ❖ *Slice the tomatoes and arrange 2 slices on each of 4 individual serving plates. Sprinkle with salt and pepper to taste. Arrange the fennel next to the tomatoes, garnish with pearl onions and parsley, and serve.* ❖ Yield: 4 servings

◄ Miniaturization has come to the salad world: red leaf and Bibb lettuces no bigger than a fist.

Miniature Corn with Mussels

◆ ◆ ◆

8 ears miniature corn

3 tablespoons butter

Coarse salt

2 pounds mussels, scrubbed

2 tablespoons chopped fresh oregano

1 pound tiny champagne grapes

Steam the corn in the husk for 3 minutes. Remove from heat, cool to room temperature, and shuck. Melt 1 tablespoon of the butter and brush on the cobs. Sprinkle with coarse salt to taste and set aside. ❖ *In a large saucepan, melt the remaining butter. Add the mussels and the oregano, cover, and cook over medium heat until all the mussels open. Drain, reserving the mussel liquor. Divide the liquor among 4 small ramequins.* ❖ *Gently pick the grapes from their stems.* ❖ *Arrange 2 ears of corn and several mussels on each of 4 individual serving plates. Garnish with champagne grapes. Serve the mussel liquor alongside.*
❖ Yield: 4 servings

....

An ear of miniature corn in all its splendor. ▲

Miniature zucchini with tiny flowers and miniature pattypan. ▶

NIGHTSHADES

Capsicum peppers, eggplant, and potatoes are related, in a rather vague way, to belladonna, or deadly nightshade, a poisonous plant. That fact inspired me to call this chapter Nightshades. What struck me as an afterthought is that it is a more than apt name for these three vegetables, since each has a sinister underside that repels as it attracts. I added artichokes to the group—let's say they're related by marriage—because of that same slightly creepy yet excited feeling I get when I ponder them.

What is the "underside" of the nightshades? Bell peppers are sweet, crunchy, and seem altogether innocent, but when I bite into one of their seeds, I'm immediately reminded of their brothers—the spice peppers—by the point of fiery hotness on my tongue. Most eggplants are purplish-black, the color of the devil's lips as depicted in fifteenth-century religious paintings. And the eggplant has a strange bitterness that must be coaxed away by flame. The artichoke's bane is obvious: such harsh leaves with little darts that draw blood from your fingertips. The inedible choke at its heart is a mean reminder of weeds and thistles in the underbrush. And the potato looks bleak and sad, despite my love for it, until it is dressed up on a plate.

So there is my Victorian thriller in vegetable terms.

Artichoke

Sweet pepper

Potato

Eggplant

◄ A terraced garden in San Miguel in Mexico. In the foreground are rows of artichoke plants.

ARTICHOKE

I suppose this is as good a place as any to admit it: when I serve artichokes to my family and friends, I examine them carefully before setting them on plates, weighing each in my hand. Then I choose the biggest, heaviest globe for myself. I can't help it; artichokes make me selfish. And now I see that my baby takes after me, yelling for each leaf to be put into his mouth so it can be clamped by his six teeth while it is pulled away.

A giant thistle that, if allowed to mature, would become a purple flower, the artichoke is a latecomer to American cuisine. Until about twenty-five years ago, it was imported from the south of France, Spain, and Italy, and tended to intimidate most American diners. These days, artichokes are grown on the coast of California and we have come to accept the hands-on experience of eating them. It has been the custom for many years to serve melted butter, hollandaise sauce, or vinaigrette in a little ramequin next to each steamed or boiled artichoke. My mother, the innovator, has come up with a superb vegetable sauce based on fresh tomatoes that beats all others. I am partial to coarse salt and olive oil if the globes are young, or a thick puree of olive paste, mushrooms, olive oil, and a touch of garlic when the globes are more mature.

Tiny artichokes, about the size of a baby's fist, can be sautéed, braised, or baked, and eaten whole, since the leaves are very tender. Their sweet, nutty flavor complements tomatoes, olives, and anchovies.

Artichoke bottoms make excellent edible containers for all manner of hors d'oeuvres and individual soufflés. Hearts, tender and meaty, can be marinated, added to vegetable mixtures, stuffed, and pureed.

A final note: Do not serve wine with artichokes. They tend to sweeten—even alter—the flavor of other foods and drink.

AVAILABILITY:
All year round; peak seasons spring and fall.

SHOPPING GUIDE:
Select globes that are heavy for their size with long stems. Avoid blackened, dried leaves, splitting and dry stems. Check stem for moistness.

STORAGE:
Will keep for 2 to 3 days, wrapped in plastic, in the vegetable drawer of the refrigerator.

Although you can't order it from a catalog, the artichoke, an edible thistle, comes in as many colors, sizes, and shapes as a child's ball.

An artichoke at its best: simply boiled and topped with its own "flower," served with a classic vinaigrette. A garnish of edible flowers in the dressing repeats the theme.

Boiled Artichokes

❖ ❖ ❖

This is a simple recipe made elegant with a "flower" created from the artichoke's heart. If you have time, you can fill the cavity with duxelles of mushrooms, a tapenade, or your favorite sauce. We like to use a mixture of salmon caviar and mascarpone, serving a vinaigrette on the side.

4 large artichokes

I lemon, cut in half

¹/₂ tablespoon salt

I cup lemon vinaigrette
(see recipe, page 269)

Using kitchen shears, trim the tips from the larger artichoke leaves. Cut the stems very short and straight across so that the artichokes will stand up when placed on a platter. Arrange the artichokes in a large saucepan, cover with water, and add the lemon halves and salt. Bring to a boil, cover and lower the heat to medium, and cook for about 25 to 30 minutes, or until a leaf can be pulled off easily. Drain and refresh under cold water and drain again, upside down. ❖ *When the artichokes have cooled to room temperature, gently spread the larger leaves apart until the lighter-colored leaves appear in the form of a cone. Carefully pull out the cone and set aside. Using a teaspoon, scrape the choke from the heart.* ❖ *Place an artichoke on each of 4 individual serving plates. Fill the heart with vinaigrette and insert the cone, point down, into the cavity. Serve with extra vinaigrette in a sauceboat.* ❖ Yield: 4 servings

SWEET PEPPER

*Being the daughter of a "woman of food,"
there was bound to be a time in my life
when eating at all became eating too
much. That period came when I was
finishing my last year of high school and
the pressures of getting accepted into a
decent university (any university, in my
case) were so great that bread and butter
and olives and a great slab of brie with a
glass of beer was a light snack to get me
through until dinnertime. By June, having
been accepted to my third-choice college
("accepted" is the important word here), I
was plump. June is not a good month to
find oneself plump at any age, and, at
seventeen, it's the worst month of all.*

*There is only one solution to getting
slender for college: the sweet pepper. This
quite ordinary vegetable, squat and green
(or yellow or red) and shiny, has an
interesting history, which I will share with
you in good time, but as a plump teenager
in June, I was more interested in what my
thinner girlfriends called "negative caloric
value," or NCV. They claimed, with
knowing smiles, that the act of chewing
sweet peppers required approximately the
same (if not a greater) number of calories
than the peppers themselves contained. I
avidly followed their advice: every day, I
ate a sweet pepper stuffed with "lo-cal"
tuna salad for lunch and munched on a
plain sweet pepper before dinner to cut my
appetite. With a bit of exercise on the side,
I lost weight quickly but there was a side
effect from the NCV peppers that my dear
friends had not mentioned. My stomach
ached and gurgled and burned for the
three weeks it took me to shed the extra
pounds. It was my mother who finally
explained to me that most people find it
difficult to digest the skin of peppers.*

*Well, thanks a lot, Mom! You could
have told me before I started to diet. To
make up for the omission, she developed a
number of low-calorie recipes using bell
peppers, either cooked or raw, with the
skins removed. From then on, whether on
a diet or not, I've enjoyed the sweet tang
of colorful peppers without suffering in
the slightest.*

*The bell, or sweet, pepper (otherwise
known as* Capsicum annuum) *comes in
more colors than a collegiate girl's ward-
robe and claims the Americas as its first
home. In the eighteenth century, the bell
pepper was adopted by southern Europe
but Americans were reluctant to partake
until about fifty years ago, when they
began to appear in produce stands. The
Dutch produce a great quantity of high-
quality bell peppers with unusual colors
like white, yellow, orange, and purple;
these are particularly sweet and tasty and
make a colorful salad when used together.*

*There are several ways to remove the
skin of a bell pepper: my favorite is to
spear it with a long-handled fork and
blacken over the flame of a gas range.
The skin then slithers off under cold
running water.*

AVAILABILITY:
All year round; peak season summer and early fall.

SHOPPING GUIDE:
Select shiny, smooth-skinned peppers with no soft
spots.

STORAGE:
Will keep for 4 to 5 days, unwrapped, in the
vegetable drawer of the refrigerator.

◀ Sweet peppers showing off their brilliant colors.

Stuffed Red Peppers with Smoked Ham

♦ ♦ ♦

This is an easy and quick appetizer for early summer when sweet, colorful peppers appear on the market. You can replace the red pepper with a yellow, orange, or purple one, or serve each guest a pepper of a different color.

2 red peppers

1 pound daikon

1 tablespoon lemon juice

2 ½ tablespoons olive oil

Salt and pepper

½ tablespoon chopped fresh parsley

12 thin slices smoked ham

Dijon-style mustard

4 slices Italian bread, toasted and buttered

Cut each pepper in half lengthwise. Remove the seeds and discard. Set the peppers aside. ❖ *Peel and julienne the daikon and transfer to a bowl. In a small bowl, mix together the lemon juice, oil, and salt and pepper to taste. Pour over the daikon, add the parsley, and toss.* ❖ *Place 1 pepper half on each of 4 individual serving plates. Fill with the daikon salad.* ❖ *Form a funnel with each slice of ham by folding back the point at the larger end. Place 3 ham "flowers" around each pepper. Serve with mustard and buttered toast.*
❖ Yield: 4 servings

....

Shredded daikon tossed with lemon juice and olive oil fills the cavity of a red pepper. With the addition of paper-thin slices of smoked ham garnished with scallions, this dish is a refreshing summertime appetizer.

POTATO

My father-in-law, Manuel Nemesio Melendez, who lives in France, hails originally from Galicia in Spain. He is a ruggedly handsome man, with piercing, dark blue eyes, a solid chin, and a roguish mustache. Although my husband claims that he was a fiery-tempered and stern father, I have always known him to be kind-hearted. Except when it comes to the question of milk and potatoes. Manuel eats potatoes twice a day, just like all other Galicians. After all, the potato was introduced to the region in the mid-sixteenth century from South America and has been avidly cultivated and eaten there ever since. Anne-Marie, his wife, my mother-in-law, obliges him by boiling up several tubers both at lunch and at dinner. Manuel peels them at the table and drizzles them with olive oil, salts them liberally and mashes them gently with a fork. He often forgoes the civet de lapin *or the tender steak set before him, preferring his* patates. *The trouble comes when Anne-Marie serves a puree. Every Frenchwoman knows that a good dish of mashed potatoes starts with riced potatoes, to which are added generous amounts of butter, salt, pepper, and milk.*

Manuel says nothing. His glare, angry and stubborn, silences all who are gathered at the table. Anne-Marie is cowed, my husband rolls his eyes, I cannot help but smile. I am, and will always be, of his camp. The best potato is naked, bejeweled with the fruitiness of a drop of olive oil and the bite of coarse salt.

But in this world, we must taste of everything. Including Anne-Marie's velvety puree, my sister-in-law's crapiaux *(rich potato pancakes with gruyère cheese), my mother's fricassee of tiny purple, yellow, and white potatoes redolent of garlic and parsley.*

Russet potatoes at an outdoor market. A quick rinse and a quick boil are all one needs to enjoy the king of vegetables.

The potato—the largest food crop in the world—is so essential, so frank, so amenable, that it stands alone as the king of the vegetable world. Its tender, starchy flesh becomes sunny when fried in butter, fluffy and sweet when baked, rich and smooth when sauced. Happily, some more unusual varieties are being reintroduced to our markets. My mother and I have enjoyed inventing recipes for them. The small, ovoid purple potato is so dark that my mother calls it black; she uses it in dishes where its odd hue can be shown off to advantage. Its flesh is dense and never mealy. Finger potatoes are simply baby "long whites"; these narrow, thumb-sized tubers have a firm flesh and, when peeled and boiled, can be served at room temperature with a dip. For a rich, buttery flavor without cholesterol, have a taste of the yellow potato. Baked, its creamy, golden flesh needs but a light sprinkling of salt and some snipped chives. It makes orange-toned French fries.

AVAILABILITY:
All year round.

SHOPPING GUIDE:
Select firm, plump tubers. Avoid sprouting eyes, soft spots, shriveled skin, and cuts.

STORAGE:
Will keep for up to 2 weeks, loosely wrapped, in an airy place at room temperature, longer at cooler temperatures. Store potatoes covered or in darkness, do *not* refrigerate.

Strains of potato from other lands are appearing in America's markets. Clockwise from top right: finger potato, russet potato, purple potato, miniature potato, and new potato.

Chinese "blanched" scallion (scallions are covered
while growing) garnishes this plate of boiled
purple potatoes. Serrano chilies and olive oil
season this beautifully hued strain of tuber.

Purple Potatoes and Blanched Scallions

◆ ◆ ◆

Blanched scallions resemble narrow, pale-yellow
ribbons. The Chinese cover the scallions while
they are growing in order to blanch them. Their
taste is mellower than regular scallions and their
unusual color enhances the purple of the potatoes. These scallions are available in Chinese
vegetable markets.

I pound purple potatoes

Salt and pepper

1/4 pound serrano chilies, seeded
and chopped

2 tablespoons olive oil

8 Chinese scallions

*Place the potatoes in a large saucepan. Cover with
water and add 1/2 teaspoon salt. Bring to a boil,
lower the heat to medium, and cook for 15 minutes or until the potatoes are done. (Purple potatoes cook much faster than regular potatoes.)
Drain and cool. Peel the potatoes, or not, as you
wish, and slice them.* ❖ *Place the potatoes in
a bowl and add the chilies and the olive oil. Season with salt and pepper to taste and toss. Garnish with strips of blanched scallions.*
❖ Yield: 4 servings

EGGPLANT

My ambivalence toward the eggplant, which I had, until recently, always called *aubergine*, in the English fashion, has quite disappeared. When I was growing up in Egypt, the Arabs prepared *al-batinjan* in many ways: fried (I hated fried eggplant— too greasy!), baked with cheese (I disliked that too), and pureed with garlic and cumin. The latter dish, called *baba ghanoush*, was the only eggplant preparation I would eat. I seldom served eggplant at home, despite my husband's clamoring for his favorite dish: *parmigiana di melanzane*, sliced eggplant baked with parmesan. For many years, Marianne and I agreed: whatever one called it, eggplant was not for us!

Then one day, as we were walking home, we saw beautiful, long purple eggplants displayed on crates in a Chinatown produce market. The color of their waxy skin, shining in the afternoon sun, was magnificent. I couldn't resist buying a bagful while Marianne grumbled. I popped them into my Chinese bamboo steamer (they were that delicate) and steamed them for about eight minutes. To my horror, their brilliant purple color turned an ugly brown! In anger and to Marianne's delight, I threw them in the garbage. A few days later, I told my story to a Chinese friend. He laughed heartily and told me to steam them for no longer than four minutes to retain their color. I tried again and succeeded. Chinese eggplants have few seeds and a sweet, smooth, tender flesh.

Marianne and I fell in love with them immediately. Yet we still bought the larger eggplants with reluctance.

A few years later, Juliette, another of my daughters, went to live in Istanbul and sent letters home filled with glowing reports about how great eggplants were! She even sent recipes she had been given by Turkish friends. Marianne and I promptly hid them away in a drawer;

Istanbul, we thought, had had a negative effect on Juliette's taste buds. Finally, I decided to check up on her and, at the same time, explore the Turkish markets, which she said rivaled any she had explored in Europe or the United States. On my first day in Istanbul, Juliette took me to her favorite restaurant. "We'll order *mezze*, Turkish appetizers. You'll love them!" and I did, including the many dishes of eggplant: fried, sautéed, marinated, cold, hot, and stuffed.

I came home, satisfied with my daughter's sense of herself and convinced that the *aubergine* was a very special vegetable. I began to experiment with the small yellow, white, and purple Italian eggplants, the long, narrow Chinese eggplant, and the small, round, green and white Thai eggplant. My greatest victory was to convince Marianne to take some home and try my new recipes. She came back a few days later, grudgingly admitting that eggplant was in fact a wonderful and versatile vegetable. Was she teasing me?

As a general rule, all kinds of eggplant varieties may be fried, sautéed, baked, or broiled. It is wise to sprinkle salt on slices of the larger ones and then drain before cooking. This removes the excess moisture that would otherwise leave them mushy.

AVAILABILITY:
All year round.

SHOPPING GUIDE:
Select firm, plump, and glossy eggplants, the smaller the better, with fresh-looking caps. Avoid eggplants with brown spots, discoloration, or bruises.

STORAGE:
Will keep for about 2 to 3 days, wrapped in plastic, in the vegetable drawer of the refrigerator. Use as soon as possible.

▲

From as far away as Thailand, Turkey, China, and Italy, and from our own backyard, the eggplant leaves its mark with a smoky-sweet taste. Clockwise from top right: Chinese eggplant, white Italian eggplant, and small and large purple eggplants.

THE OUTSIDERS

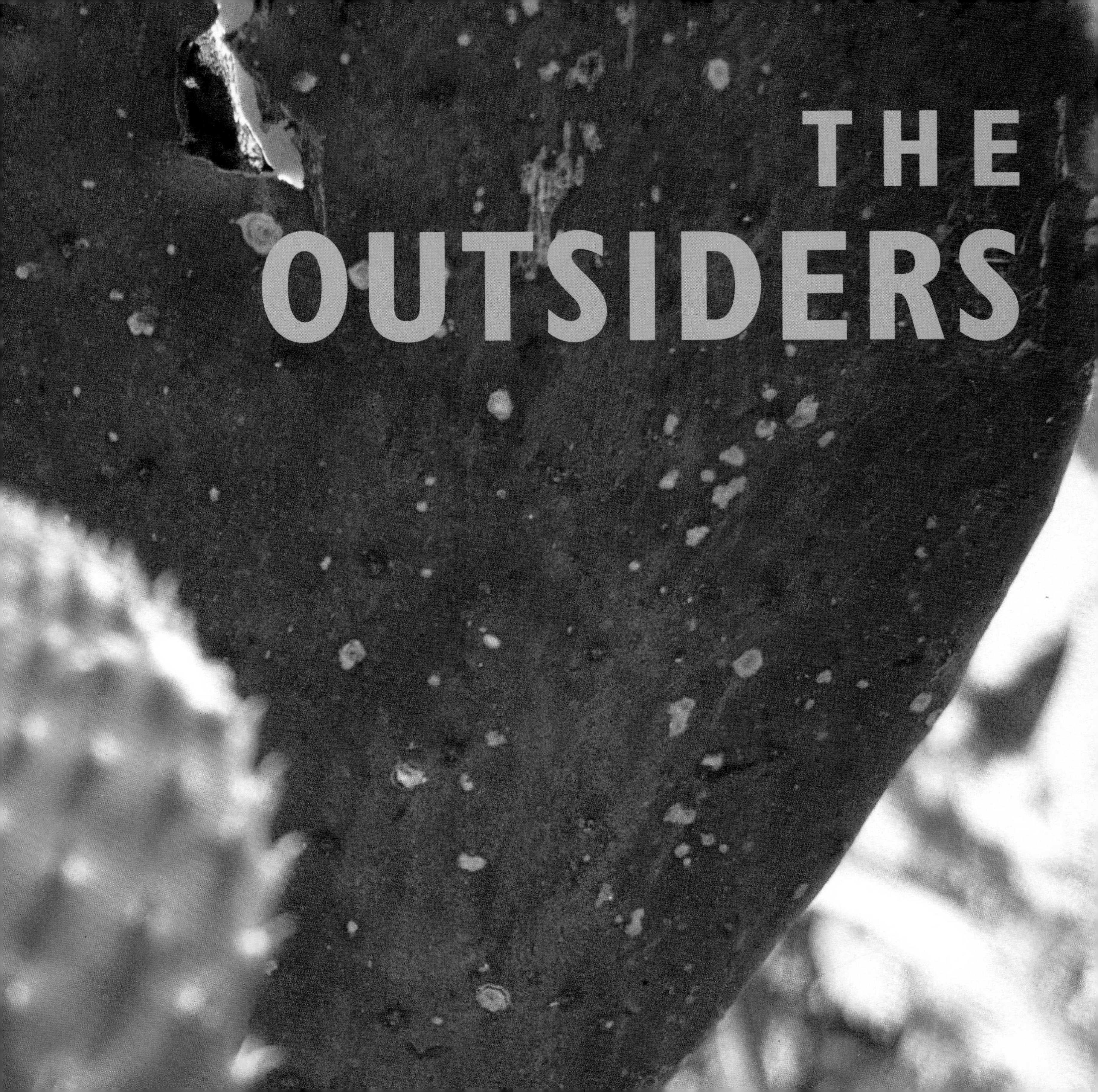

The vegetables in this chapter are an odd lot. They don't seem to fit into any particular category yet they are quite possibly the most captivating of all the vegetables we chose to discuss. In a sense, they represent the aim of this book: to bring light to the complexities and variances of the vegetable world. After all, who thinks of cactus leaves as a food to be venerated? And who grew up eating the youngest shoots of ferns (fiddleheads) or the stalks of a perennial (artichokes)? By coming to accept and embrace these plants as culinary diamonds in the rough, Colette and I learned that the vegetable world is limitless, and ever-evolving. Romanesco cauliflower is a perfect example: the melding of two separate yet similar vegetables into a work of art.

Finally, we realized that vegetables have their own quirks and eccentricities that must be respected. If okra hides a gelatinous substance in its heart, then we will simply refrain from cutting it. If cardoons have prickles and strings, then we will handle them gently. And if salicornia has a salty character, then we will pair it with sweet-fleshed foods.

Listen to your vegetables: even if they're strangers to you, let them in.

Cardoon

Romanesco
cauliflower

Fiddlehead fern

Salicornia

Cactus leaf

Okra

◀ A cactus garden outside of San Miguel, Mexico.

CARDOON

When Marianne was a little girl, her favorite book was *Winnie-the-Pooh*. I read her a chapter every night before she went to sleep. Every time we'd get to the part when Eeyore, the donkey, ate thistles, Marianne would yell "Gross!" I would remind her then that she loved thistles, too.

The cardoon, like the artichoke, is an edible thistle popular in Mediterranean countries; only recently has it appeared in American markets. Marianne especially liked cardoons prepared by my own mother, who would keep only the inner leaves and heart, trim them of strings and prickles, cut them into strips, and serve them raw with a sauce of melted butter, olive oil, garlic, and anchovies.

The cardoon is a winter plant and delicious when boiled and served with butter, cream, or freshly grated parmesan; in soup; sautéed with clams or oysters; fried in a batter; gratinéed; or in a salad with tiny black olives.

Resembling celery, cardoon stalks, ranging in length from one to five feet, are deeply ridged and prickly around the edges. When preparing cardoons, have a bowl of cold acidulated water at hand; like the artichoke, the cardoon will blacken if left exposed to the air.

To cook cardoons, blanch them in boiling water with one tablespoon lemon juice for about fifteen minutes. Then refresh them under cold running water. You can then lightly peel the stalks and remove the strings. Try substituting celery in the following recipe when cardoons are not available.

AVAILABILITY:
December to March.

STORAGE:
Will keep for about 10 days, wrapped in plastic, in the refrigerator.

SHOPPING GUIDE:
Select short, firm, young-looking stalks. If discolored or brown at the top, trim away before cooking.

Despite their prickly and stringy outer leaves, cardoons are thistles that reveal a tender heart.

Like a dinosaur thistle, cardoons grow tall and weedy in the corner of a West Coast garden. ▶

Braised Cardoons
with Clementines

* * *

Okay: I admit it. Sometimes I doubt my mother. As she was caramelizing the clementines and braising the cardoons, I said "Ick." I've never been more wrong. Glazed, the sweet, juicy clementines, with their covering of sugar that crackles just so, are a perfect foil for slightly bitter, herbed cardoons. Serve them with a cold, dry white wine.

1 medium cardoon (about 2 pounds)

Juice of 1 lemon

4 tablespoons butter

Salt and pepper

1 teaspoon dried sage

4 clementines or mandarin oranges

³⁄₄ cup sugar

1 tablespoon chopped fresh parsley

Cut each stalk of the cardoon into 1 ¹⁄₂ -inch pieces and halve the thicker pieces. In a large saucepan, bring 2 quarts of water to a boil with 1 tablespoon of the lemon juice. Add the cardoon pieces and lower the heat to medium. Cook the cardoons for 15 minutes. Drain and refresh under cold water. Drain again. Remove any visible strings from the cardoon pieces and peel. ❖ *In a saucepan, melt the butter. When the butter is foamy, add the cardoon pieces, 1 tablespoon of the lemon juice, salt and pepper to taste, and the sage. Lower the heat to medium, cover, and cook for 30 to 40 minutes, or until tender.* ❖ *Meanwhile, cut each clementine in half across and remove any pits. In a heavy saucepan, melt the sugar with ¹⁄₄ cup water. Just before the sugar begins to color, add the clementine halves, 4 at a time, and cook for 5 minutes, turning once so that they are glazed all over. Transfer with a slotted spoon onto a sheet of aluminum foil. Continue until all the clementines are glazed.* ❖ *Arrange the clementines and cardoons on a serving platter. Sprinkle with chopped parsley and serve.* ❖ Yield: 4 servings

Litchis sweeten these slightly bitter sautéed cardoons, accompanied by caramelized clementines topped with caviar—a perfect play of contrasts.

ROMANESCO CAULIFLOWER

This might make her cross, but my mother has trouble with cauliflower in the kitchen. Perhaps its awkward shape puts her off, or the way the florets don't break apart evenly, or its color, a "sort of" white. She's into drama, I think, and prefers intensity and assertiveness in a vegetable. A cauliflower just sits there.

That's why I was thrilled when she dragged me, as soon as I entered the house, into her temple of creation (i.e., the kitchen) to show me a new kind of cauli-flower. "Romanesco," she said breath-lessly. I thought she was describing, in a fake Italian accent, the cauliflower's shape: a swirling cone of opalescent green made up of many smaller cone-shaped florets, like curls on the innocent head of a cherub. "It's from California, a cross between broccoli and cauliflower. It's called Romanesco. Isn't it gorgeous!"

I had to admit it was beautiful. But—a doubting Thomas, I—could she overcome her trouble with cauliflower in the kitchen? That evening, she served squid-ink pasta with tiny Romanesco cones and pink pickled garlic. My doubts were squelched after just one taste, but I was in a playful mood. "Why not make this dish with regular cauliflower?" I asked not-so-innocently. My mother smiled. "Parce que je suis née une princesse, et le choufleur, c'est pour les paysans comme toi!" (Because I was born a princess, and cauliflower is for peasants like you!) Touché, Mom!

Proof that mixed heritage gives birth to beautiful children. A cross between broccoli and cauli-flower, the magnificent Romanesco is shown here in its miniature and regular sizes.

AVAILABILITY:
September to November.

SHOPPING GUIDE:
Select very tight heads with a bright, lime-green color and outer leaves. Avoid heads with florets that are bruised or spotted with black.

STORAGE:
Will keep for 7 days, wrapped in plastic, in the vegetable drawer of the refrigerator.

Green and White Soup

• • •

1 small Romanesco cauliflower

1 medium white cauliflower

6 cups chicken broth

4 tablespoons butter

Salt and pepper

½ tablespoon rum

Hot-pepper sauce

2 tablespoons finely grated lime zest

1 beet, cooked and sliced, for garnish (optional)

Using a small, sharp knife, separate the Romanesco and white cauliflower into small florets. ❖ *Steam the cauliflower and Romanesco florets until tender, about 12 to 15 minutes.* ❖ *Transfer the cauliflower and Romanesco and 2 cups of the chicken broth to the bowl of a food processor and puree. Pour the puree into a saucepan. Add the remaining broth and heat slowly, stirring constantly. Add the butter and correct the seasoning with salt and pepper to taste. Add the rum and a dash of hot-pepper sauce. Bring to a boil and turn off the heat.* ❖ *Divide the soup among 4 serving bowls. Sprinkle with lime zest and garnish each bowl with a beet slice (if desired). Serve immediately.* ❖ Yield: 4 servings

White and Romanesco cauliflower are blended to create this creamy, lime-spiked soup. A setting sun of sliced beet with a sprig of rosemary garnishes this bowl.

Tiny Romanesco Cones
with Squid-Ink Pasta

◆ ◆ ◆

1 cup hazelnuts

½ pound (2 sticks) butter, at
room temperature

Salt and pepper

1 Romanesco cauliflower

2 tablespoons vegetable oil

1 pound fresh squid-ink pasta

½ cup grated parmesan cheese

12 cloves pink garlic*

2 tablespoons chopped fresh parsley

*Pink garlic is available in Japanese grocery stores. The garlic is
blanched, then pickled in vinegar and beet juice.

Preheat the oven to 400 degrees.
❖ *Spread the hazelnuts on a cookie sheet and toast
in the oven for a few minutes, then allow to cool. In a
saucepan, bring 1 quart of water to a boil, add the hazelnuts, bring back to a boil, and immediately turn off
the heat. Drain and refresh the nuts under cold water
and rub off the skins. Pat dry with paper towels.* ❖
*Place the hazelnuts and 1 tablespoon of water in the
bowl of a food processor and puree. Add the butter and
puree well. Transfer to a bowl, and add salt and pepper to taste.* ❖ *Steam the Romanesco, whole, until
barely tender, about 6 minutes. Remove from the heat,
cover, and set aside.* ❖ *In a 3-quart saucepan, bring
2 quarts of water to a boil. Add ½ tablespoon salt and
the oil. Add the pasta, bring back to a boil, and cook
for 4 minutes, or until tender. Drain. Place the pasta
on a round serving platter. Add half the hazelnut butter and toss well.* ❖ *Separate the Romanesco florets
and place in a bowl. Add the remaining hazelnut butter
and the parmesan and toss.* ❖ *Divide the pasta among
4 individual serving plates. Place some florets on one
side, garnish each plate with 3 garlic cloves, sprinkle
with chopped parsley, and serve.*
❖ *Yield: 4 servings*

Squid-ink pasta, steamed Romanesco, and pink
pickled garlic repeat the dramatic colors of the
orchid. In our recipe, they are tossed with
hazelnut butter.

Romanesco with Fried Smelts

◆ ◆ ◆

If you use frozen smelts, defrost one hour before frying. This dish is delicious when served with a dry white wine and hot Italian or French bread.

I large Romanesco cauliflower

I pound fresh or frozen smelts

2 cups flour

Salt and pepper

Oil for frying

Italian flat-leaf parsley sprigs for garnish

1/4 cup extra-virgin olive oil

3 cloves garlic, peeled and sliced

Steam the Romanesco, whole, for 8 minutes, or until barely tender. Turn off the heat, cover, and set aside. ❖ *Pat dry the smelts with a paper towel.* ❖ *Pour the flour into a paper bag along with salt and pepper to taste. Add the smelts, close the bag, and shake well until the smelts are coated with flour.* ❖ *Fill a deep-fryer to its capacity with oil and heat to 360 degrees.* ❖ *When the oil is hot, fry half the smelts until golden brown. Using a spatula, transfer the smelts onto paper towels, then place them on a plate in a very low oven to keep warm. Repeat with remaining fish.* ❖ *Place the Romanesco in the center of a round serving platter. Surround with the fried smelts, tails facing out. Garnish with sprigs of parsley.* ❖ *In a small saucepan, heat the olive oil over medium heat. Add the garlic and sauté until golden. Add some parsley sprigs and salt and pepper to taste. Remove immediately from the heat and pour over the Romanesco.* ❖ Yield: 4 servings

Crispy, deep-fried smelts are served with a whole Romanesco.

FIDDLEHEAD FERN

When Marianne was barely a year old, we spent the month of July on Canada's Prince Edward Island. We elected to stay, as paying guests, with the Connaughs, an Irish family who owned a lovely colonial farmhouse set in the middle of rolling fields. My strongest memory of that sojourn had to do with food. Breakfast was the best—and largest—meal of the day: we were served homegrown oats cooked for hours on a wood-burning stove, farm-fresh eggs, delectable heavy cream, sweet butter, hot scones, and scrumptious jam. (I gained close to eight pounds in a month.) Marianne was an adorable baby (if I may say so myself) and was quickly adopted by Siobhan, the farmer's wife. The three of us would do chores and take walks together. One morning, Siobhan asked if I would like to go fiddlehead-picking. Noticing my puzzled expression, she explained that fiddleheads were the tips of ostrich ferns gathered just after they sprouted and before they unfurled their feathery leaves.

The fiddleheads grew on the banks of a small river that crossed the property. There were thousands of ferns, about eight inches high, balancing their tips in the breeze. I was told not to pull the plant but to gently cut the tip with a knife. I plopped Marianne on the grass and, with an eye on her and a basket at my feet, I started to cut the young shoots. Within minutes I had a basket full of fiddleheads, some loosely covered with fuzzy brown leaves as if they were emerging from a cocoon. I caught Marianne putting one in her mouth and tried to stop her. "It's all right, dearie," said Siobhan. "You can eat them raw."

Back at the house, Siobhan soaked the fiddleheads in cold water, shaking them from time to time to remove the brown leaves. Then she washed them under cold running water until they looked

like small, brightly colored green pinwheels.

That night we partook of fiddlehead soup. The flavor of fiddleheads falls somewhere between asparagus and artichokes. The next day, we ate sautéed fiddleheads and a fiddlehead salad. Each dish was delicate, tasty, and unusual.

Years later, fiddleheads began to appear on the menus of some of America's more adventurous chefs. Today, from the end of April to the end of July, fiddleheads can be found in open farmers markets and in specialty produce stores.

It was at the Greenmarket in New York's Union Square that I met John Grozinski, a young farmer who sells fiddleheads. I often go in early June, after a good rain, to his farm in Cochecton Center, New York, to help pick them. As on Prince Edward Island, they grow along the banks of a stream that flows through his property. However, John does not believe in eating them raw, as they might be carcinogenic. When he sells them

at the market, he patiently explains to interested shoppers what they are and how to cook them.

We urge those who pick fiddleheads in the forest or along river banks to make absolutely sure, by looking at photographs before going to pick them, that they are from the ostrich fern.

AVAILABILITY:
April to July.

SHOPPING GUIDE:
Select small fiddleheads (1 1/2 to 2 inches in diameter) with tightly rolled, bright green, firm coils. Avoid those with thick tails, a sign of toughness.

STORAGE:
Will keep for 1 to 2 days, in a sealed plastic bag, in the vegetable drawer of the refrigerator. Best eaten the day they are bought.

Fiddleheads with Rice Noodles

• • •

3 tablespoons butter

I pound fiddleheads, washed and picked over

I pound small white mushroom caps,
wiped clean

Salt and pepper

I tablespoon chopped fresh tarragon or
I teaspoon dried tarragon

¼ pound transparent Chinese rice noodles,
soaked in hot water for 20 minutes

½ tablespoon olive oil

In a large skillet, melt the butter. When the butter is hot, add the fiddleheads and mushroom caps. Cook over medium heat for 3 to 4 minutes, stirring constantly. Sprinkle with salt and pepper to taste and add the tarragon. Mix well and set aside. ❖ *Drain the noodles. Place in a bowl and toss with the olive oil and salt and pepper to taste.* ❖ *Arrange some noodles on each of 4 individual serving plates, top with fiddleheads and mushrooms, and serve.* ❖ *Yield: 4 servings*

....

▲ Chinese rice noodles are topped with sautéed fiddleheads and mushroom caps. Black sesame seeds are used as garnish.

◀ A close look at the fiddlehead. It is vital to be familiar with its physical aspect before setting out to pick it in the wild. Other fern-tips may be toxic or poisonous.

These fiddleheads are ready to be cut—not pulled—from the ground, rinsed, and sautéed in a bit of butter for a wild and delicious treat. ◀◀

SALICORNIA

When I was living in Paris, I would let my husband sleep late on Sundays so that I could do the week's food shopping in peace at the outdoor market on the avenue in front of our building. I stuffed bills and coins into a little leather change purse (a handbag is out of the question in a crowded marché), *put my arm through the handle of my net bag, and set out to peer at (never touch!), choose, and pay for the freshest produce, meat, and fish this side of Rungis. I had my favorite vendors: a Jewish fruit seller who always tried to guess my heritage and my age; a dairymaid, originally from Cantal, who took pains to find me the ripest camembert; and a fishmonger who knew that I preferred to clean my fish at home and was always amused by this. It was he who introduced me to* pousse-pied—*what my mother calls salicornia—a dark green, jointed, delicate plant. He told me it would make the perfect bed for the salmon trout I had just purchased, provided I blanched and rinsed it first. I did as I was told and reveled in the salty, crunchy, briny plant. Of course: I was eating seaweed!*

And that is what I thought it was until my husband and I came back to the United States. My mother explained that, although salicornia tastes distinctly of the sea, it grows in marshes and along sea coasts and not *under the water.*

Why is it called pousse-pied *(push-foot) in French? According to the authority I admire most, Elizabeth Schneider, the name is a corruption of* perce-pierre *(rock-piercer), coming from the fact that the plant grows in cliff crevices. I have my own theory, however.* Pousse-pied *is also the name of a flat-bottomed boat that is used to navigate in shallow or marshy water and is pushed with the foot. The proximity of the plant to the boat leads me to believe that one simply borrowed its name from the other (the boat was probably used to collect the plant).*

Whichever name you choose, remember that salicornia has a short and variable season, sometimes in the summer. Trim away the root and part of the stem, if thick. Toss the salicornia raw into salads, or steam and serve it as a bed for all manner of fish.

Salicornia, the briny-flavored marsh plant that makes a crunchy bed for fish and seafood.

AVAILABILITY:
June to September.

SHOPPING GUIDE:
Select small and young-looking shoots. Avoid dark or soft spots and slime.

STORAGE:
Will keep for 2 to 3 days, wrapped in paper towels, in the vegetable drawer of the refrigerator.

Lightly sautéed salicornia is topped with lime zest and served with crab salad.

Salicornia with Lobster or Crab Salad

• • •

This dish can be served as a main course for lunch or as an appetizer for dinner. Serve with hot buttermilk biscuits and a cold Chardonnay.

1 pound salicornia

2 tablespoons butter

Salt and pepper

1 pound lobster or crab meat, picked over

2 medium potatoes, cooked and diced

4 scallions, trimmed and thinly sliced

1¼ cups lemony mayonnaise
(see recipe, page 269)

Trim the stems off the salicornia; rinse and pat dry.
❖ *In a skillet, melt the butter. Add the salicornia and salt and pepper to taste and sauté for 2 minutes over medium heat. The vegetable should remain crisp and undercooked. Transfer to a bowl.*
❖ *In another bowl, combine the lobster meat, potatoes, and scallions. Add the mayonnaise and toss well. Correct the seasoning.* ❖ *Arrange the salicornia on a serving platter along with the lobster or crab salad.* ❖ *Yield: 4 servings*

CACTUS LEAF

Montse Pecanins is a Mexican sculptor who is also an excellent cook. It was at her house that I first tasted cactus-leaf salad. I always thought that cacti were plants that you admired from afar, since their sharp needles are quite uninviting. Her salad, therefore—cool, lemony, and crunchy—was a real surprise.

On a trip to San Miguel de Allende in Mexico, I saw women in the market scraping cactus leaves with knives. I bought some and tried Montse's salad at home. To Montse's recipe (her secret is a teaspoon of baking soda to preserve the bright green of the leaves) I added red peppers for color and a touch of coriander for more bite. Cactus salad makes a refreshing side dish for hamburgers or fried chicken.

AVAILABILITY:
All year round.

SHOPPING GUIDE:
Select firm, bright green leaves. Avoid those with blemishes or soft spots.

STORAGE:
Will keep for 2 to 3 days, in a sealed plastic bag, in the vegetable drawer of the refrigerator.

A peasant woman scraping cactus leaves at a farmers market in San Miguel, Mexico.

Cactus leaves are widely used in Mexican cuisine.

Red pepper and onion are tossed with blanched
and julienned cactus leaves in this Mexicó-inspired,
tangy salad, served with a chilled rosé.

Cactus Salad with Red Peppers

• • •

1 teaspoon baking soda

2 large fresh cactus leaves

1 tablespoon lemon or lime juice

3 tablespoons olive oil

Salt and pepper

1 teaspoon chopped fresh coriander

1 medium onion, peeled and thinly sliced

1 red pepper, seeded and diced

*In a saucepan, combine the baking soda with 1
quart of water and bring to a boil. Add the cactus
leaves and blanch for 2 to 3 minutes. Drain and
refresh under cold running water. Drain again and
pat dry. Julienne the cactus leaves and place in a
salad bowl.* ❖ *In a small bowl, combine the
lemon juice, oil, salt and pepper to taste, and the
coriander. Mix well. Add the sliced onion and diced
red pepper to the cactus. Pour the dressing over the
salad, toss, and serve.* ❖ Yield: 4 servings

....

OKRA

My mother, whose freezer contains ice, ice cream, a couple of Japanese dumplings, and that's all, once used to buy those small cardboard boxes wrapped with paper that contain cut-up frozen okra. She didn't buy frozen peas or string beans or corn. No, we ate those vegetables fresh when I was a little girl. She bought in the frozen state the only, the one and only, vegetable that all four of her children detested equally. What's worse, she would take the okra out of the box (ripping up the paper so that she couldn't follow the cooking directions), put the frost-glued green things in two inches of water, bring them to a boil, drain them and—oh, horror—serve them as is. The cause of our disgust (there is no nicer word) was the goo, the slime, the clear, mucilaginous stuff that oozed out from the pods. We couldn't understand how grown-ups actually ingested slime, and swore that we would never stoop so low. So we whined our way through dinner, and the okra was tossed into the garbage, untouched.

Each of my mother's four children maintained an ongoing hatred of that poor vegetable and three still harbor that aversion to this day. The fourth has come to terms with okra. I now love it.

I was living in Brooklyn, New York, and had invited some friends to brunch when I first spied okra in its natural state. The fresh pods, tiny, bright green, and touched with dew, had just come in from the Bronx Terminal Market to my neighborhood greengrocer. I delighted in their shape: gently ridged and curving cones with pert little stems. I was feeling particularly adventurous and bought a pound. But how to prevent the dreaded slime from contaminating my guests' plates? Then it hit me. If kept whole, the pods would retain the mucilage.

As an aside, I must communicate a very important, not-to-be-forgotten tip: if in doubt about how to prepare a vegetable, sauté it with garlic and parsley.

The brunch was a complete success. We began with homemade, chunky applesauce (dark, grade-B maple syrup gave it complexity) and slices of walnut bread. I then served soft-scrambled eggs (only a double boiler and heavy cream will do), Canadian bacon, sautéed okra redolent of parsley and garlic (do not forget my tip!), and semolina bread. Despite the large quantity of champagne downed by my guests, they were all pleasantly surprised by the tender pods, al dente and sweet, with the garlic as a piquant foil. I was in love for good.

The moral is: pick 'em young and cook 'em whole. Of course, a classic gumbo needs okra's slime (it is a magical soup thickener) and some grown-ups seem to relish it. Young okra can be gently steamed and served with a pat of sweet butter, or sautéed with all manner of other vegetables, such as tomatoes, cucumbers, peppers, and onions. It is particularly delicious boiled and tossed with a dressing of olive oil, lemon, and fresh tarragon.

Marianne is all wrong. I know how to cook okra and always did, but when fresh okra was not readily available, I did *occasionally* buy frozen okra. Of course, frozen okra doesn't compare to the fresh okra I remembered from my childhood: so sweet and tender, you'd forget the slime. But I got her message soon enough and stopped buying those boxes after a while. But she doesn't remember that!

I went back to serving okra after one of my visits to Japan, when I tasted the best okra dish I had ever had. Composed of sliced okra, garlic, and mountain yam, it had the consistency of ratatouille and was served over thin slices of roast pork. When I looked for okra in my local vegetable market, I was pleased to find that farmers had finally decided to pick it young.

Okra can differ not only in size but in color too: from bright green to pinkish purple. I experimented and came up with new recipes like spicy okra soup with shredded beets and steamed, sliced okra napped with olive oil and seasoned with hot pepper and cumin. I was even able to duplicate the Japanese okra sauce. Today, I serve it with broiled quail or fresh roast ham. I don't know if Marianne approves of my recipes. I never cook okra when she's around, since she always brings up my okra dishes of years ago. She never gives me a break. I'll give her one thing, though: she makes the best gumbo north of Louisiana.

AVAILABILITY:
All year round; best in early summer.

SHOPPING GUIDE:
Select fresh-looking young okra (some varieties are larger than others, so ask your greengrocer). Avoid pods with dark blemishes or signs of mold.

STORAGE:
Will keep for 1 to 2 days, wrapped in a paper bag, in the vegetable drawer of the refrigerator.

Steamed Okra with Tamarillo

✦ ✦ ✦

Tamarillo, also called tree tomato, is a lovely, egg-shaped fruit with a satiny purple or yellow skin. Its bittersweet taste is reminiscent of a not-quite-ripe tomato mixed with honey. When using tamarillo, be sure to peel it; the skin can be excessively bitter. Tamarillo can be eaten raw in a vegetable salad, baked and served with pork or duck, or stewed with fruit and nuts as a topping for ice cream or sliced fresh pineapple.

I pound small okra

I tablespoon olive oil

Juice of I lime

I clove garlic, peeled and slivered

Salt and pepper

4 tamarillos, peeled*

I tablespoon sugar

½ tablespoon chopped fresh chives

*To peel tamarillos without crushing the flesh, dip for I minute in boiling water, refresh under cold water, and drain. The skin will slip off easily.

Trim the okra and steam for a few minutes, until tender. Place in a bowl and add the olive oil, I teaspoon of the lime juice, the garlic, and salt and pepper to taste. Mix well and set aside. ❖ *Thinly slice the tamarillos. Sprinkle with sugar and I teaspoon of the lime juice. Toss and set aside.* ❖ *To serve, place the okra on a round serving platter. Garnish with the sliced tamarillos and sprinkle with the chopped chives.* ❖ Yield: 4 servings

A dramatic arrangement of whole, steamed okra and sliced tamarillo.

FRUIT AS
VEGETABLE

I *don't have a single filling in my mouth. My mother has one that she got when she was pregnant for the third time. Each of my sisters has two, and my brother has three. I don't know how many my father has; he plays hooky from the dentist three times a year and never, never opens up his mouth wide enough for a good look. There's no secret to our dental success: as children, we ate little candy, no cake, and no soda. The sweetest tidbit we enjoyed was an occasional chocolate chip cookie. Dessert was always fruit.*

It is no surprise, then, that I balked at my mother's frequent suggestions of using fruit in savory dishes. Adding pomegranate seeds to braised beef was, to me, like pouring chocolate sauce on a hamburger. But she didn't stop. In fact, I think she enjoyed making me cringe.

In the end, my mother won. A rare occurrence, yes, but sometimes it just had to happen that way. When we were looking for a splash of brilliant color, a mellow accent to counterbalance bitter or grassy overtones, an element of surprise in an otherwise traditional composition, my mother opted for fruit. I would shake my head mournfully. Then I would look at a sunset-colored pool of mango puree framing the sails of a quartered braised onion; at a shell of pink guava holding the pearls of a brown rice salad; at pale yellow stars of carambola lighting up a dish of cranberry beans. And I would smile as I tasted each treasure.

Fruit's sugar, as I came to understand, is so tied to flavor and perfume that it can be manipulated until it is not truly "sweet." Certain cuisines— Oriental, Catalan, British—are partially based on this fact, so that we find red dates simmered with chicken and mushrooms, grapes added to braised herring,

Pomegranate

Guava

Prickly pear

Plantain

◄ Tamarillo, at left, also known as tree tomato, is a bitter fruit from Central and South America, perfect as a foil for grilled meats. Feijoa, similar in size and shape and hailing from the same countries, is sweeter and more palatable when raw.

calves' liver napped with orange sauce. But instead of using common fruit, we opted for exotica, finding ourselves seduced by magnificent colors and unusual flavors. Tamarillo and prickly pear, passion fruit and persimmon, red bananas and green figs—these are just a few of the many fruits that my mother and I now use in our daily cooking of savory dishes.

We always use fruit that is at its peak of flavor (green bananas or plantains are the only exception) but not overripe. I find that some herbs clash with tropical fruits; among them are caraway, dill, and chives. It is wise, as well, to think carefully of the dessert you will serve when using fruit as vegetable. A cake flavored with vanilla, cinnamon, rum, or nuts is a good choice; even I am known to shun fruit after a meal prepared with fruit. But I won't eat that cake, either. I still have two more kids to go before I'm allowed to have a cavity!

Prickly pears are so named because of the tiny cactus needles in the rind that are difficult to remove from the skin. It is wise to don rubber gloves while peeling them. ▶

Pork Tenderloin with Pomegranate Seeds

◆ ◆ ◆

2 1-pound pork tenderloins

3 cloves garlic, peeled and thinly sliced

Salt and pepper

2 cups beef broth

2 tablespoons soy sauce

1 tablespoon fresh thyme leaves

2 pomegranates, seeded*

*When seeding a pomegranate, first rub your hands with lemon juice to prevent staining.

Preheat the oven to 325 degrees.

❖ *Prick the tenderloins with a sharp knife and insert slivers of garlic. Sprinkle each with salt and pepper to taste and place them in a baking dish with the broth. Brush the tops with the soy sauce, sprinkle with thyme, and bake for 1 hour, basting occasionally. Remove from the oven and keep warm on top of the stove.* ❖ *Just before serving, pour the pan juices into a small saucepan, add the pomegranate seeds, and simmer for 5 minutes.* ❖ *Slice the pork and arrange on a serving platter. Pour the sauce over the meat and serve.*

❖ Yield: 4 servings

The pomegranate is a daunting foe, as its rubylike seeds are difficult to pry from their secure clusters. Well worth the effort, the sweet-sour seeds make tasty and unusual garnishes.

Guavas Stuffed with Brown Rice

. . .

Guavas are usually served as a fruit—chopped in fruit salads or stewed. We like to stuff them with leftover chicken or ham or, as here, with rice as a vegetarian dish. For those who are not vegetarian, you can garnish stuffed guavas with smoked ham.

12 ripe guavas

4 cups chicken broth

1 tablespoon vegetable oil

1 cup brown rice (not instant)

Salt and pepper

1 tablespoon chopped fresh coriander

1 sweet red pepper, chopped

1/4 pound dried cranberries

12 slices smoked ham or turkey

Dijon-type mustard

Peel the guavas and slice off about 1 inch from the tops. Using a small spoon, carefully scoop out the seeds. ❖ *In a large saucepan, bring the chicken broth to a boil. Add the guavas and cook for 5 minutes, or until barely tender. Using a slotted spoon, transfer to a serving platter and keep warm. Reserve the broth.* ❖ *In a saucepan, heat the oil. Add the rice, stir until the rice is coated, and cook for 1 minute. Then add 2 1/2 cups of the reserved broth and salt and pepper to taste. Bring to a boil, lower the heat, and simmer until all the broth is absorbed, about 35 minutes. If the rice is still hard, add another 1/2 cup of broth and cook until tender.* ❖ *Adjust the seasoning and add the coriander and the sweet pepper. Mix well. Stuff the guavas with the rice mixture.* ❖ *Place 1 tablespoon of dried cranberries on each slice of ham. Roll the ham to enclose the cranberries.* ❖

Place the ham rolls between the stuffed guavas, garnish with the remaining cranberries, and serve. ❖ Yield: 6 servings

Guava shells are stuffed with brown rice and served with sliced baked Virginia ham. Tart dried cranberries cut the sweetness of the brown rice.

Prickly Pears with Squid Salad

• • •

1 pound cleaned squid, washed,
trimmed, and sliced

5 peppercorns

1 bay leaf

Salt and pepper

Juice of 1 lemon

1 ½ tablespoons olive oil

1 green pepper, diced

1 teaspoon dried thyme

1 small onion, diced

4 small artichokes, cooked

3 prickly pears, peeled and sliced

Place the squid in a saucepan and add 3 cups of boiling water, the peppercorns, bay leaf, and salt to taste. Bring to a boil, lower the heat, and simmer for 4 minutes. Drain. ❖ *Place the squid in a bowl and add the lemon juice, oil, green pepper, thyme, and onion. Mix well and correct the seasoning.* ❖ *Remove most of the leaves from the artichokes. Cut 1 inch off the top of the remaining leaves. Cut each artichoke in half and remove the choke. Sprinkle with salt and pepper.* ❖ *Arrange the squid salad in the center of an oblong platter and surround it with the artichoke halves on one side and the sliced prickly pears on the other.* ❖ Yield: 4 servings

Prickly pears and baby artichokes complement a salad of squid tossed with green peppers and vinaigrette.

PLANTAIN

If my mother considers herself to be part Japanese, through the careful yet instinctive absorption of Japanese culture and cuisine, then I might be so bold as to claim Guatemala as part of my own cultural make-up. It all began when the whole family traveled to Central America for the summer. I was thirteen. Lake Atitlán, at the base of a volcano, shimmered in the heat of the long afternoons and the Indians smiled as they sold honey-sweet figs and tiny bananas. So taken was I with their grace and ink-black hair, with their colorful weaving and dusty-brown feet, that I braided my own hair with wide red ribbons, wrapped a woven skirt around my waist, and went barefoot everywhere. Plantains were plentiful in the markets: sweet, firm, and fragrant. We ate them as tostones *(fried rounds), in stews, braised, and sautéed in butter and honey and served with thick cream. I was very disappointed that, when we returned to the "other" life in Manhattan, plantains were not readily available.*

Then I grew up, moved across the river to Brooklyn, and heard the sweet sounds of Spanish once again. The markets near my house featured plantains in all their stages of ripeness: green and starchy, yellow and tender, black and sweet. But here there were other bananas as well: burro, manzana, *and* red banana. *I wasn't sure how to prepare these so I conferred with my mother and we did a little research together. This is what we found out:*

- *The plantain is a berry; its plant is an herb gone nuts (you can't sprinkle it over soup, though!)*

- *Sometimes the banana will not ripen but becomes hard instead. It is therefore important to press the flesh of a blackened plantain; if it does not yield slightly, it should be thrown out.*

- *The plantain should not be refrigerated.*

- *The* manzana *is a tiny, fat, green plantain that is very good fried.*

- *The* burro *is a large, green plantain with a lot of starch, suitable for stews.*

- *The red banana is sweeter than any other plantain variety, perfect for desserts.*

AVAILABILITY:
All year round.

SHOPPING GUIDE:
Select plantains with unblemished skins and fresh-looking stem ends that are underripe; allow them to ripen at room temperature.

STORAGE:
Will keep at room temperature until fully ripened. Do *not* refrigerate; freeze when ripe, if desired.

▲ The plantain and its cousins, the red banana and the fat, tiny *manzana.*

Plantains Stuffed with Minced Veal

◆ ◆ ◆

4 green plantains

Salt and pepper

1 pound chopped veal

1 egg

2 cloves garlic, peeled and minced

1 teaspoon finely chopped fresh thyme

Pinch of cumin

1 tablespoon sesame oil

1 tablespoon vegetable oil

1 bunch Chinese chives (2 ounces)

1 lemon, cut in wedges

Boil the unpeeled plantains in 2 quarts of salted water for 10 minutes, or until tender but not overcooked. Drain and refresh under cold water. ❖ *Halve each plantain lengthwise and remove a 2-inch-wide wedge from the center of each half. Discard the wedge.* ❖ *Preheat the oven to 350 degrees.* ❖ *In a bowl, mix together the veal, egg, garlic, thyme, cumin, and sesame oil. Season with salt and pepper to taste. Fill each trough with the veal mixture. Brush with oil.* ❖ *Bake the plantains in a buttered baking dish for 15 minutes, or until veal is golden brown.* ❖ *Line a serving platter with the chives. Place the stuffed plantains on top and serve with lemon wedges.* ❖ *Yield: 4 servings*

Chopped veal, seasoned with thyme, garlic, and cumin, stuffs a plantain. A bunch of Chinese chives forms a bed for this unusual main course.

APPENDIX

Avocado-Ginger Sauce

...

1 medium ripe avocado

2-inch piece fresh ginger, peeled
and sliced

1 tablespoon chopped fresh coriander

1/2 cup olive oil

Juice of 1/2 lemon

Salt and pepper

Cumin

Peel and quarter the avocado. ❖ *Place the avocado, ginger, coriander, olive oil, and lemon juice in the bowl of a food processor and puree until smooth. Transfer to a bowl and add salt and pepper to taste and a pinch of cumin. Mix well and correct the seasoning.* ❖ *The sauce will keep for several days in a tightly sealed container in the refrigerator.* ❖ *Yield: 1 1/2 cups*

....

Avocado-Tomatillo Sauce

...

1 pound tomatillos

1 medium ripe avocado

Cumin

1 tablespoon lemon juice

2 tablespoons olive oil

Salt and pepper

Remove the husks from the tomatillos. Place the tomatillos in a saucepan and cover with water. Bring to a boil, lower the heat, and simmer for 5 minutes, or until tender. Drain. ❖ *Peel and quarter the avocado. Place the avocado pieces, the tomatillos, a pinch of cumin, lemon juice, and olive oil in the bowl of a food processor and puree until smooth.* ❖ *Pour the sauce into a bowl. Correct the seasoning with salt and pepper to taste and refrigerate until ready to use. The sauce will keep for several days in a tightly sealed container in the refrigerator.* ❖ *Yield: 2 cups*

....

Carrot Sauce

...

1 pound carrots, scraped and cut into
1-inch pieces

4 cups chicken broth

Salt and pepper

Cumin

2 tablespoons sour cream

1 tablespoon minced fresh mint

Place the carrots in a saucepan, add the broth, bring to a boil, and cook for 20 minutes, or until the carrots are tender. Drain the carrots, reserving the liquid. ❖ *Puree the carrots with 1/2 cup of the reserved liquid. (If the sauce is too thick, add more broth.) Add the salt and pepper to taste, a pinch of cumin, the sour cream, and mint.* ❖ *Serve at room temperature.* ❖ *Yield: 2 cups*

....

Carrot Sauce with Tofu

...

4 carrots, scraped and cut into
1-inch pieces

Salt and pepper

1 16-ounce cake soft tofu

1/2 tablespoon lemon juice

1 tablespoon olive oil

1 tablespoon chopped fresh basil

Hot red-pepper flakes

Place the carrots in a saucepan, cover with water, add 1/2 teaspoon salt, and bring to a boil. Lower the heat and cook for 20 minutes, uncovered, or until tender. Drain. ❖ *Place the carrots, tofu, lemon juice, and oil in the bowl of a food processor and puree. Transfer to a bowl and add the basil, salt and pepper, and pepper flakes to taste.* ❖ *This sauce will keep for several days in a tightly sealed container in the refrigerator. Reheat gently before serving.* ❖ *Yield: 2 cups*

....

Ginger Sauce

...

4 scallions, trimmed and cut into
1-inch pieces

3-inch piece fresh ginger,
peeled and sliced

1 garlic clove, peeled

1/2 teaspoon sesame oil

1/4 cup peanut oil

Salt and pepper

Place the scallions, ginger, and garlic in the bowl of a food processor. Process until finely chopped. Add the sesame and peanut oils and process for 30 seconds. Pour into a bowl. Add salt and pepper to taste. ❖ *This sauce will keep for several days in a tightly sealed container in the refrigerator.* ❖ *Yield: 1 1/2 cups*

....

Horseradish Mousse

...

A good sauce to serve with Chinese long beans or braised cardoons.

2 cups heavy cream

Salt

1 tablespoon prepared horseradish

1 tablespoon chopped fresh chives

Beat the cream with a pinch of salt until stiff. Carefully fold in the horseradish. Sprinkle with chives and serve. ❖ *Yield: 2 cups*

....

Lemon Sauce

• • •

The tart taste of this lemon sauce will enhance a veal or pork roast or a poached fish.

3 cups chicken broth

3 tablespoons lemon juice

I tablespoon fresh tarragon leaves

8 tablespoons (I stick) butter,
cut into small pieces

Salt and pepper

In a saucepan, bring the broth to a boil. Add the lemon juice and tarragon and continue to boil until the broth has reduced to I cup. ❖ *Pour the broth into the bowl of a food processor and, with the machine running, add the butter, I tablespoon at a time. The sauce should be creamy.* ❖ *Transfer to a bowl and add salt and pepper to taste.*
❖ Yield: 2 cups

....

Lemon Vinaigrette

• • •

2 tablespoons lemon juice

6 tablespoons olive oil

$\frac{1}{2}$ teaspoon salt

$\frac{1}{2}$ teaspoon Dijon-style mustard

Freshly ground pepper

I teaspoon chopped fresh tarragon
leaves (optional)

Combine all the ingredients in the bowl of a food processor and process for 30 seconds. Or combine all the ingredients in a bowl and beat with a fork for I minute, until mixed thoroughly. ❖ Yield: $\frac{1}{2}$ cup

....

Lemony Mayonnaise

• • •

This mayonnaise is made in a food processor. By adding different herbs or spices, you can make the mayonnaise green or pink.

2 egg yolks

2 cups vegetable oil

Juice of I lemon

Salt and pepper

Place the egg yolks in the bowl of a food processor. Process for 4 seconds, until frothy. ❖ *With the food processor running, slowly add the oil, pouring in a very thin stream until the mixture thickens. Continue until I $\frac{3}{4}$ cups of the oil have been used. Slowly add the lemon juice, then the remaining oil.* ❖ *Transfer the mayonnaise to a bowl. Add salt and pepper to taste and mix well.* ❖ Yield: 3 cups

Green Mayonnaise

5 spinach leaves and 8 sprigs parsley
or
5 spinach leaves and 2 sprigs dill
or
$\frac{1}{4}$ pound watercress ($\frac{1}{2}$ bunch)

I tablespoon fresh tarragon leaves

I recipe Lemony Mayonnaise (above)

Place the spinach or watercress and specified herb in the bowl of a food processor with 4 tablespoons of Lemony Mayonnaise and puree. Blend this mayonnaise into the remaining Lemony Mayonnaise. Refrigerate until ready to serve. ❖ Yield: 3 cups

Pink Mayonnaise

I teaspoon tomato paste
or
5 sundried tomatoes
or
I teaspoon paprika

I recipe Lemony Mayonnaise (above)

Place the tomato paste, sundried tomatoes, or paprika in the bowl of a food processor with 4 tablespoons of Lemony Mayonnaise and puree. Blend into the remaining mayonnaise. Refrigerate until ready to serve. ❖ *These mayonnaises will keep for at least a week in a tightly sealed container in the refrigerator.* ❖ Yield: 3 cups

....

Okra Sauce

• • •

This sauce is excellent with fresh roast pork, broiled quail, or striped bass.

$\frac{1}{2}$ pound small okra

I clove garlic, peeled and finely chopped

3-inch piece mountain yam*

I tablespoon light soy sauce

Salt and pepper

Lemon juice

*A Japanese potato, available in Japanese grocery stores. You can substitute jícama.

Wash the okra and trim the stems. Blanch in boiling water for 2 minutes. Drain and coarsely chop. Transfer to a bowl, add the garlic, and mix well. ❖ *Peel the mountain yam and finely grate over the okra. Add soy sauce and salt and pepper to taste. Mix well. Add a few drops of lemon juice, mix again, and refrigerate until ready to serve.* ❖ Yield: I cup

....

Onion Sauce

• • •

3 tablespoons butter

3 large onions, peeled and minced

$\frac{1}{2}$ cup dry white wine

Salt and pepper

In a large skillet, melt the butter. When the butter is hot, add the minced onions, lower the heat, and cook for 5 minutes. Add the white wine and simmer for 10 minutes, stirring from time to time, or until the onions are soft and transparent. Do not brown. Season with salt and pepper to taste. Keep at room temperature until ready to serve. ❖ Yield: 2 $\frac{1}{2}$ cups

....

Parsley Sauce

• • •

1 1/2 cups parsley, washed and
trimmed (1 bunch)

1 cup Chinese or garlic chives
(1 bunch)

1 cup chicken broth

Salt and pepper

2 tablespoons vegetable oil

Place the parsley, Chinese chives, broth, and salt and pepper to taste in the bowl of a food processor and puree. ❖ *Transfer the mixture to a saucepan and bring to a boil. Remove from the heat and cool. Correct the seasoning. Mix in the oil just before serving.* ❖
Yield: 2 cups

....

Pâte Brisée

• • •

This dough is very easy to make in a food processor. The secret to its success is well-chilled butter. The dough will keep for several days refrigerated. It can even be frozen.

1 3/4 cups flour

8 tablespoons (1 stick) butter, chilled
and cut in pieces

1/4 teaspoon salt

1 egg

1 tablespoon oil

1/4 cup ice water

Combine the flour, butter, and salt in the bowl of a food processor. Process for 20 seconds, or until the mixture forms a coarse meal. ❖ *In a small pitcher, combine the egg, oil, and ice water. While the food processor is running, pour the egg mixture through the feed tube. As soon as the liquid is used, turn off the food processor and remove the dough. Form a ball, wrap in wax paper, and chill in the refrigerator for 1 hour, or until firm.* ❖
Yield: 1 9-inch pie shell

....

Fresh Pea Puree

• • •

2 cups fresh peas
(about 2 pounds in the pod)

Salt and pepper

2 large potatoes

1 cup chicken broth

2 tablespoons butter

2 tablespoons chopped fresh sage

Place the peas in a saucepan, cover with boiling water, add 1/2 teaspoon salt, and bring to a boil, uncovered. Lower the heat to medium and cook for 5 minutes. Drain and set aside. ❖ *Peel the potatoes and quarter. Place the potatoes in a saucepan, cover with boiling water, and cook for 15 minutes. Drain.* ❖ *Place the peas and potatoes with some of the chicken broth in the bowl of a food processor and puree. Transfer to a bowl and add more broth if the puree is too thick. Add the butter and season with salt and pepper to taste and the sage. Mix well and serve.* ❖ *Yield: 4 servings*

....

Red Pepper Sauce

• • •

In the winter you can use tangerine shells as a container for this sauce. The scarlet sauce is striking— like a tropical sunset—when set against the orange of the tangerine. Allow one per person. Cut the tangerines in half across and carefully remove the flesh. Squeeze the tangerine flesh and use the juice in place of the orange juice in the recipe.

2 large sweet red peppers

1/4 cup orange juice

Salt and pepper

Quarter the peppers and remove the seeds. Place in a saucepan and cover with water. Bring to a boil, lower the heat, and cook for 10 minutes uncovered. Drain. Puree the peppers in a food processor with the orange juice. Transfer to a bowl and season with salt and pepper to taste. Keep warm until ready to serve. ❖ *This sauce will keep for several days in a tightly sealed container in the refrigerator.* ❖ *Yield: 2 cups*

....

Rouille

• • •

2 thick slices French baguette, cut up

5 cloves garlic

1/2 teaspoon hot red-pepper flakes,
or less, if desired

1/2 teaspoon salt

3 tablespoons olive oil, or more
as needed

Soak the bread in 1/4 cup cold water for 5 minutes, then squeeze dry with your hands. Place the bread and the remaining ingredients in the bowl of a food processor. Process until well combined, then add more oil, drop by drop, until the mixture is thick and emulsified. If the rouille separates, add more soaked bread and process until smooth. ❖ *Yield: 1/2 cup*

....

Tomato Coulis

• • •

This sauce is excellent over fresh pasta, with stuffed summer squash, or with fish or poultry.

1 14-ounce can whole tomatoes
in their juice

2 tablespoons tomato paste

6 black Greek olives, pitted

Salt and pepper

1 tablespoon lemon juice

3 tablespoons olive oil

1 tablespoon any chopped fresh herb

Drain, quarter, and seed the tomatoes. Place in the bowl of a food processor, add the tomato paste and black olives, and puree. Transfer to a bowl and refrigerate for several hours. Using a spoon, remove most of the water on the surface. Add salt and pepper to taste, lemon juice, and olive oil. Add the fresh herbs and mix well. ❖ *Refrigerate until ready to serve.* ❖ *Yield: 2 1/2 cups*

....

Coulis of Watercress

• • •

This is an excellent sauce to serve with fish or pork.

1 ½ pounds watercress (3 bunches)

½ cup olive oil

Juice of ½ lemon

Salt and pepper

2 tablespoons heavy cream

Trim off and discard the stems of the watercress. Rinse and drain the leaves. Place in a saucepan, cover with water, and bring to a boil. Boil for 5 minutes, uncovered, turn off the heat, drain, and cool. ❖ *When the watercress is cool to the touch, squeeze out as much of the water as possible. Place in the bowl of a food processor, add the oil and lemon juice, and puree. Pour into a bowl and correct the seasoning with salt and pepper to taste. Just before serving, beat in the cream.* ❖ Yield: 2 cups

....

Zucchini-Wasabi Sauce

• • •

½ pound fresh spinach

2 medium zucchini, cut into
2-inch pieces

3 tablespoons soy sauce

½ teaspoon prepared wasabi*

Salt and pepper

*Japanese powdered horseradish. Available in Japanese and Korean grocery stores.

Trim and discard the spinach stems. Place the spinach and all the other ingredients in the bowl of a food processor, add 3 tablespoons water, and puree. Transfer to a bowl. Correct the seasoning with salt and pepper to taste. Refrigerate until ready to serve. ❖ *This sauce will keep for several days in a sealed container in the refrigerator.* ❖ Yield: 2 cups

....